"For those of us who, scholars or not, are interested in the complex engagements of psychoanalysis, it can be frustrating how poorly psychoanalysis has been understood in terms of both its theories and practices. Then, too, there's the brutally reductive matter of its popular cultural representations. These simplistic ideas are not only harmful to those who would like to grasp psychoanalysis intellectually, but to analysands' experience of psychoanalysis in the consulting room. A book that describes the wide range of heterogeneous possibilities that have emerged from this form of encounter would therefore be a welcome intervention – one that can deepen and expand our sense of psychoanalytic practice in ways that work to enrich its theoretical underpinnings as well."

Dr Devorah Baum, *Associate Professor of English Literature and Critical Theory, University of Southampton, UK*

"There has been a distinct lack of suitable academic literature offering tangible clinical examples of the unique features of a Lacanian analysis. Hence I am confident this book would be well received and read with great interest by academics in the social sciences and humanities alike, as well as the wide range of clinicians working in the mental health field. Over the decades a number of myths have emerged around the image of the Lacanian analyst, playing on a cliched stereotype of the Lacanian style of interpretation. These myths are quite misleading and urgently in need of challenge; there is no doubt that they have negatively influenced the reception of Lacanian analysis more broadly across the UK. This volume would address these misconceptions in a way that should, I hope, make the key precepts of contemporary Lacanian technique accessible to a wider audience."

Dr Gwion Jones, *Assistant Professor in Psychology, Coventry University, UK*

I0094013

How Does Analysis Work?

How Does Analysis Work? uses short, compelling vignettes from people in Lacanian analysis to explore how analytic interpretation works.

Insights, revelations, connections, meanings and non-meanings all feature in these anonymous accounts of crucial moments in analysis, providing a sense of what it is all about. Drawn from a wide range of analysands, some seasoned analysts and others just starting out, these vignettes show how change takes place. The short pieces are drawn from Lacanian analysis, but many go against cliched views of what Lacanians do in their work, spanning both the classical and the radically innovative and showing the use of humour and theatre in psychoanalytic practice.

How Does Analysis Work? will be of great interest to psychoanalysts and Lacanian analysts in practice and in training, as well as anyone who is curious about the analytic process.

Berjanet Jazani is a medical doctor and practicing psychoanalyst based in London, UK. She is the president of the College of Psychoanalysts (UK), clinical member of the Centre for Freudian Analysis and Research (CFAR), and the author of *Lacanian Psychoanalysis from Clinic to Culture*; *Lacan, Mortality, Life and Language: Clinical and Cultural Explorations*; and *The Perfume of Soul from Freud to Lacan: A Critical Reading of Smelling, Breathing and Subjectivity* (all Routledge).

The Centre for Freudian Analysis and Research Library (CFAR)

Series Editors: Anouchka Grose, Darian Leader, Kristina Valendinova

CFAR was founded in 1985 with the aim of developing Freudian and Lacanian psychoanalysis in the UK. Lacan's rereading and rethinking of Freud had been neglected in the Anglophone world, despite its important implications for the theory and practice of psychoanalysis. Today, this situation is changing, with a lively culture of training groups, seminars, conferences and publications.

CFAR offers both introductory and advanced courses in psychoanalysis, as well as a clinical training programme in Lacanian psychoanalysis. It can provide access to Lacanian psychoanalysts working in the UK and has links with Lacanian groups across the world. The CFAR Library aims to make classic Lacanian texts available in English for the first time, as well as publishing original research in the Lacanian field.

Critique of Psychoanalytic Reason
Studies in Lacanian Theory and Practice
Dany Nobus

What Can We Know About Sex?
A Lacanian Study of Sex and Gender
Gisèle Chaboudez

What Does It Mean to Make Love?
A Psychoanalytic Study of Sexuality and Phantasy
Gérard Pommier

How Does Analysis Work?
Examples of Lacanian Interpretation
Edited by Berjanet Jazani

www.cfar.org.uk
https://www.routledge.com/The-Centre-for-Freudian-Analysis-and-Research-Library/book-series/KARNACCFARL

How Does Analysis Work?

Examples of Lacanian Interpretation

Edited by Berjanet Jazani

Routledge
Taylor & Francis Group

LONDON AND NEW YORK

Designed cover image: Getty | dogayusufdokdok

First published 2025
by Routledge
4 Park Square, Milton Park, Abingdon, Oxon, OX14 4RN

and by Routledge
605 Third Avenue, New York, NY 10158

Routledge is an imprint of the Taylor & Francis Group, an informa business

British Library Cataloguing-in-Publication Data
A catalogue record for this book is available from the British Library

ISBN: 978-1-032-63770-9 (hbk)
ISBN: 978-1-032-63766-2 (pbk)
ISBN: 978-1-032-63772-3 (ebk)

DOI: 10.4324/9781032637723

Typeset in Times New Roman
by codeMantra

To Khosro Fravahar, who hears me beyond the couch.

Contents

Contributors

Camille Germanos Al Hasan is practising psychoanalysis in London with Centre for Freudian Analysis and Research (CFAR) training. Her PhD research at Goldsmiths University is on language, AI and psychoanalysis, where she is affiliated with the Centre for Philosophy and Critical thought (CPCT). She serves at the Foundation for Art and Psychoanalysis for the development of an Oral History Collection and printed publications.

Farhad Anklesaria graduated with degrees in Sociology and International Studies from Yale College in 2010. He has since been a consultant in New York and an educator in India. Currently, he is a clinical trainee at the CFAR in London.

Arturo Bandinelli is a London-based filmmaker and psychoanalyst in formation at the CFAR. His written publications include 'What Does the App Want?' (*Psychoanalysis, Culture and Society*, 2021), 'Knowledge and Truth in Contemporary Society: A Psychoanalytic Investigation of the "Post-Truth Era"' (*Awry: Journal of Critical Psychology*, 2022), and "Creative Disruption with/in Psychoanalysis: On Forgetfulness and Stupidity" (in *Creative Disruptions Psychosocial Scholarship as Praxis*, Palgrave Psychosocial Series, 2024).

Adela Bass graduated in Medicine from the Universidade Federal de Ciencias da Saude de Porto Alegre, Brazil, in 1971. She obtained an MSc in Medical Demography from the London School of Hygiene and Tropical Medicine in 1977 and an MA in Psychoanalysis from the Middlesex University London. She is a candidate of psychoanalysis at CFAR.

Sabine Bauer holds a PhD in Modern Literature. She's an associate member of CFAR and a member of the Forum of London affiliated with the International of the Forums of the School of Psychoanalysis of the Forums of the Lacanian Field (IF-SPFLF) – an International Federation of Forums based in Paris. She is currently the international delegate of the Forum of London.

Florence Boyd is an artist and illustrator living in Cardiff, currently taking time to focus on being a mother. She is in psychoanalytic training at CFAR.

Marie-Laure Bromley-Davenport is trained with the Institute of Group Analysis and the Philadelphia Association and is a member of CFAR.

Marcus Coelen is a psychoanalyst and psychoanalytic supervisor in Berlin and New York. He is an affiliated professor of Comparative Literature and Romance Philology at the University of Munich. He is the editor of a book series called Neue Subjektile with the Viennese publishing house Turia+Kant offering titles at the intersections of poetic thought, psychoanalysis, and philosophy.

John Conolly began his psychology studies from a Humanities background in modern languages and literature. He worked just under ten years as an organisational psychologist before training with CFAR. He has taught at the Tavistock and Portman NHS Trust, Middlesex University, Mental Health Department, while a counsellor at a central London NHS service for homeless people; which he has now led for the past 15 years. He now enjoys his North London private practice 'Psyharmonia', his family and walking his little dog 'Marley'!

Ariana Cziffra is a psychoanalyst, artist and translator. She has been practising psychoanalysis in Mauritius for 17 years. She is an affiliate member of CFAR in London and is involved with several Lacanian organisations and study groups abroad.

Vincent Dachy is a psychoanalyst in the Lacanian orientation. He is a member of CFAR and World Association of Psychoanalysis (WAP). He has been practising in London and teaching psychoanalysis for over 30 years.

Livia De Marco is a psychotherapist and trainee psychoanalyst at CFAR. She has done some studies in Literature and Music.

Nicolas Duchenne is a psychoanalyst working in London. He is a member of the London Society of the New Lacanian School and on the UKCP registered training of the Guild of Psychotherapists.

Mark Elmer is a practising psychotherapist since 1993 working in charities and National health service (NHS) settings. Currently, he is the chair of trustees at Philadelphia Association.

Hilda Fernandez-Alvarez practices Lacanian psychoanalysis in Vancouver, Canada. She co-founded the Lacan Salon in 2007 and currently serves as its clinical director. She has published various articles and book chapters on the theory and practice of psychotherapy and psychoanalysis, looking at the entwinement between the social and the individual.

Julie Fotheringham, formerly a professional dancer, is a psychoanalyst practicing in New York City where she is a member of Das Unbehagen.

Lakis Georghiou is a healthcare professional, clinical teacher and psychoanalytic psychotherapist. He is interested in the coercions of heteronormative constructs within a Patriarchal world as well as reconfiguring his own personal perspective on gender within Contemporary Psychoanalysis.

Patricia Gherovici is a practising psychoanalyst and author. She is founding member and director of Philadelphia Lacan Study Group and Seminar.

Yannis Grammatopoulos is a Lacanian psychoanalyst originally from Greece. He pursued his undergraduate studies in psychology at Panteion University in Athens, furthering his education with postgraduate and doctoral studies in London. He obtained an MSc in Applied Psychology from Brunel University and completed his PhD in Psychoanalysis at Middlesex University. He is a member of British Psychoanalytical Society (BPS), United Kingdom council for psychotherapy (UKCP), the Guild of Psychotherapists, the Association of Greek Psychologists, and the Hellenic Society of the New Lacanian School.

Anouchka Grose is an Australian-British author and a practising psychoanalyst in London. Her recent books include *Fashion: A Manifesto* and *Eco-Anxiety*.

Daniela Oliveira Grund is a psychoanalyst in formation at the CFAR. She practices in London, has worked for mental health institutions in the UK and is a welcomer at Bubble & Speak, a 'Maison Verte' style drop-in for small children and their carers.

Loryn Hatch is a psychoanalyst and clinical psychologist in New York City. She is affiliated with Apres-Coup and Pulsion psychoanalytic institutes as an analysand, analyst and supervisor.

Owen Hewitson practices psychoanalytic psychotherapy in London, UK. He trained at the Guild of Psychotherapists and obtained his PhD in Psychoanalysis from Middlesex University. He writes about psychoanalysis in various publications, on LacanOnline.com, and speaks about psychoanalysis in the UK and internationally.

Françoise Higson is a psychoanalytic psychotherapist in London, working in private practice and the NHS. She is a psychoanalyst in formation at the CFAR.

Andrew Hill is a practising psychoanalyst and a member of the CFAR.

Cara Caddick Hinkson is a candidate on the clinical training programme at the CFAR.

Annabel Hollick lives and works in Cambridge. She is a practising psychoanalyst, full member of the CFAR and currently holds the position of Honorary Secretary of the College of Psychoanalysts, UK.

Luis Izcovich is a psychiatrist, psychoanalyst and founding member of the International School of the Forum of Lacanian field. He has taught in the Department of Psychoanalysis of the University of Paris VIII. He currently teaches psychoanalysis at the Clinical College of Paris.

Berjanet Jazani is an author, medical doctor and practising psychoanalyst based in London. She is the president of the College of Psychoanalysts, UK, and a member of CFAR. Her recent books include *The Perfume of Soul from Freud to Lacan: Olfaction, Breathing and Subjectivity* (2024) and *Lacan, Mortality, Life and Language: Cultural and Clinical Explorations* (2021).

Phoebe Jeffery is a psychoanalytic psychotherapist in training at the Guild of Psychotherapists, London, UK.

Robert Jeffery is undertaking psychoanalytic clinical training at the CFAR in London.

Matt Johnson is a clinician and independent researcher. He holds degrees from Amherst College and New York University and practices privately in New York City, specialising in work with adolescents. He is currently a member of the teaching faculty at the Pulsion International Institute of Psychoanalysis and Psychoanalytic Psychosomatics.

Hannah Joll is a therapist in private practice and a trainee at CFAR.

Gwion Jones has worked in private practice as a psychoanalyst for over 30 years. He is an active member of CFAR and vice chair of the Council of Psychoanalysis and Jungian Analysis. In addition, he is assistant professor at Coventry University, teaching in the School of Health.

Rick Koster is in psychoanalytic formation at CFAR. His musical career as a violinist has ranged from playing Beethoven and Bartok as a member of the Duke Quartet. He has also played on numerous film scores such as *Barbie* and *Mission Impossible* and can often be heard leading the orchestra of the Lion King show in the West End.

Darian Leader is an author, psychoanalyst and founding member of the CFAR. His recent books include *Is It Ever Just Sex?* and *Juissance: Sexuality, Suffering and Satisfaction.*

Robert Leake is on the psychoanalytic clinical training programme at the CFAR.

Henrik. E. Lynggaard is a London-based clinical psychologist and Lacanian psychoanalyst in formation with CFAR. Henrik worked for more than 25 years in the NHS with people affected with learning disabilities and autism. He is the co-author of the book *Learning Disabilities: A Systemic Approach* (Karnac, 2006).

Fanis Lyrintzis is an assistant lecturer and PhD candidate at the Business School of Essex University. His doctoral research focuses on resistance in the workplace, immigrant labour, precarious work and workers' subjectivity. His research interests include Psychoanalysis, Philosophy, and Politics.

Stefan Marianski is a psychoanalyst in formation. He is a service manager at the Psychosis Therapy Project and learning manager at the Freud Museum London."

Alex Martin studied at the Centre for Research in Modern European Philosophy (CRMEP) and is currently doing the Introductory Course at the CFAR. He teaches Philosophy and Politics and works for the Independent Workers' Union of Great Britain (IWGB).

Yaprak Ölmez is a British Association for Counselling and Psychotherapy (BACP)-accredited psychotherapist, and she is currently completing her formation as a psychoanalyst at CFAR. She has over 12 years of experience in working with children, young people and adults with various mental health difficulties in the NHS and therapeutic community settings.

Carol Owens is a psychoanalyst and Lacanian scholar in Dublin, Ireland. Her books include *Psychoanalysing Ambivalence with Freud and Lacan: On and Off the couch* (with Stephanie Swales, 2020, Routledge) and *Psychoanalysis and the Small Screen: The Year the Cinemas Closed* (with Sarah Meehan O'Callaghan, 2023, Routledge).

Sinziana Ravini is a Swedish-Romanian writer, journalist and psychoanalyst based in France. She is general Secretary of the patient association Ariane-Paris linked to the Department of Adult Psychiatry of the Pitié Salpêtrière University Hospitals where she also conducts group therapy. She also co-hosts the psychoanalysis seminar 'Cliniques et Critiques' at the Ménagerie de Verre.

Jonathan Ridley is a psychoanalytic psychotherapist based in London. He is a member of United Kingdom Council for Psychotherapy (UKCP) and the Guild of Psychotherapist.

Diego Semerene is Assistant Professor of queer and transgender media at the University of Amsterdam and co-founder of the Queer Analysis Research Group at the Amsterdam School of Cultural Analysis (ASCA). Most recent publications include 'Embarrassing Subjects, Undisplayable Objects: Of Impossible Encounters Between Trans and Cis That Have Nonetheless Taken Place' and 'Ejaculative Kinship in the Age of Normative Data Flows'.

Juana Cavaliere Silva is a psychoanalyst practising in London. She is a member of CFAR, College of Psychoanalysts UK (CP-UK) and the Lcanian School and New Lacanian School (LS-NLS). She is also a clinical psychologist trained in Brazil.

Vanessa Sinclair, PsyD, is a psychoanalyst based in Sweden and the host of Rendering Unconscious Podcast. Some of her books include *Psychoanalytic Perspectives on the Films of Ingmar Bergman: From Freud to Lacan and Beyond* (Routledge, 2023), *The Pathways of the Heart* (Trapart Books, 2021), *Scansion in Psychoanalysis and Art: The Cut in Creation* (Routledge, 2020), *Switching Mirrors* (Trapart Books, 2019) and *Rendering Unconscious: Psychoanalytic Perspectives, Politics & Poetry* (Trapart Books, 2019).

Gerry Sullivan is a practising psychoanalyst and a member of CFAR.

Laura Tarsia is a psychoanalyst working with adults and children. She is a member and lecturer at CFAR. She is currently living and practising in Singapore.

Ginny Thomas has a background in art and is a psychoanalyst and writer working in Cambridge. She is a member of CFAR, the Guild of Psychotherapists and the College of Psychoanalysts, UK.

Sam Tierney studied Philosophy at Kingston University (Centre for Research in Modern European Philosophy – CRMEP) and currently attends CFAR's Psychoanalytic Studies programme. He is an intermittent artist and has worked as a teacher.

Kristina Valendinova is a psychoanalyst living and working in London. She's a member of CFAR in London and the Cercle Freudien in Paris, and a co-founder of Bubble & Speak, a drop-in centre for small children and their carers.

Eve Watson, PhD, is involved in psychoanalytic practice, training, education and research in Dublin (Ireland). She has published over 30 essays on psychoanalysis, sexuality, film, culture and literature. Her co-edited book is *Clinical Encounters in Sexuality: Psychoanalytic Practice and Queer Theory* (Punctum Books, 2017). She is the academic director of the Freud Lacan institute (FLi), Dublin, and is the editor of *Lacunae, the International Journal for Lacanian Psychoanalysis*.

Jamieson Webster is a psychoanalyst in New York City. She teaches at the New School for Social Research and is on the board of Pulsion Institute. Her last book was *Disorganisation and Sex* (Divided, 2022).

Anne Worthington is a psychoanalyst practising in South London. She is a member of CFAR, the College of Psychoanalysts, UK, and the Guild of Psychotherapists.

Carmen Wright is a psychoanalyst, writer and member of the CFAR, where she sometimes teaches. She also works with infants and carers at 'Bubble & Speak', a Françoise Dolto-inspired Maison Verte. She is based in London.

Astrid Zecena is a psychoanalyst working with adults and children in North London. She is also a mother of two girls who remind her it is not only the analysts who can help us see what we normally cannot!

Acknowledgements

We all have stories that we need to get through life. Each story is individually created, whether we love it or hate it. However, the fabric to weave or concoct a personal tale comes from a social bond. In an encounter with the Other, which may involve a single narrative or an action, we might form an unconscious interpretation. Using this particular interpretation, our life journey begins. When our unique story fails to translate the meaning of life for us, we look for a safe space to go over the plot once again, to share it and to analyse every little part of it.

When we are ready to share all those intimate personal moments, vague memories, the pain of losses, regrets and much more, we might also wonder how being heard can possibly introduce change.

In an analytic setting, the voices (and the silences) from the couch find a destination where they can be carefully listened to and, above all, respected. What is heard might then leave a mark, a mark which can only be identified retrospectively, almost always in the form of a testimony. This invisible mark involves not so much the question of some visible change with which our contemporary culture is so obsessed, but a mark that becomes a new fabric for a new story or a missing part of a story line.

I was honoured to be part of the courageous and sincere sharing of personal stories of analysis from the contributors to this collection. Each and every one of these testimonies of an analytic journey is respected and appreciated.

The last year was a year of change for me personally, confronting me with impossible challenges. Working on this collection was not possible without my Khosro's support and love. A special thank you with a little bunch of Edelweiss to you!

I would like to express my sincere thanks to my friend Darian Leader who suggested the project, initially back in 2018. It took a good six years to make this collection happen!

A big thank you to Susannah Frearson and Saloni Singhania from Routledge whose help has always been appreciated.

To the memory of my father and to my beautiful mother whose presence in my life is constant, generous and invaluable.

I would like to thank you, Bernadette, Barsian and Bardia, for being with me unconditionally, and to everyone else whose help I have received in the past year for the work on this book project.

A special thanks to my friends and colleagues Anne Worthington, Andrew Hodgkiss, Pat Blackett, Mary Horlock, Kalpa Rao, Denis and Nina Nedelyaev, Francesca Silvani, John Osbourne, Sepideh Pourkoushki, Andreea Goloca, Albana and Mary Artemi.

And finally, to Arthur Nabat.

Introduction

'Does analysis work at all?', a sceptical financial adviser seeking consultation for his autistic child asked me a few years ago. His question is ever present in my mind when I see a new analysand or face a challenge in analytical work, and I often hear the perplexity expressed by his question repeated in various narratives in the consulting room. Many people start analysis with doubts and concerns as to the efficacy of the analytic method. They often wonder: 'Is it the right treatment for me?'

A keen interest in such questions is often a sign that a person is ready to gain something from analysis. Psychoanalysis, as a fruit of late 19th-century European culture, was originally a way of listening to a subject's account of their suffering in order to make sense of it, discover the reason for it and treat it, if it was susceptible to treatment. Being sceptical is a way to enter and potentially remain in analysis. Beginning with scepticism, the work continues by way of Socratic questioning. To give an example: a patient felt himself hindered on all sides by something overwhelmingly present in his everyday life, stealing every possible source of pleasure, like poison ivy. Arriving in the analyst's consulting room, his first remark was that he had exhausted every possible treatment, including psychoanalysis, in years of searching for a remedy to his suffering, which was a particular form of obsession. His symptom returned again and again, haunting him like a ghost. Having despaired of a cure from doctors and therapists, he had attempted complete seclusion as a possible treatment, but to no avail. Why then had he chosen to try psychoanalysis once more? His answer was: 'I have come in order to prove that psychoanalysis does not work!' 'To be the proof?', the analyst asked. 'Yes!', he replied. 'For who?', the analyst asked again. And the work began.

Freud initially conceptualised analytic interpretation in the 1890s as a way of retrieving the patient's memories from apparent oblivion. So the theory of analytic interpretation starts from remembering and 'un-repressing' the repressed. Then, from *The Interpretation of Dreams* (Freud, 1899) onwards, his attention turned decisively to the universality of symbols and meanings. When interpretation begins to decode meaning in order to make use of representations in dreams and other unconscious formations (such as a lapsus or a bungled action), it comes up against the wall of resistance. Analysands with some knowledge of psychoanalytic technique have often carried out the extensive interpretations of their symptom before they came to see a psychoanalyst, but with little effect. What makes such knowledge different when it is produced in the consulting room?

In his article of 1913, 'On Beginning the Treatment', Freud drew a parallel between the beginning of analytic treatment and the start of a game of chess (Freud, 1913).

A chess player has several options for opening the game, but will try to choose moves that put them at an advantage, so that eventually he or she will win and there will be no further moves to be made. A psychoanalysis is not a competitive game, but it also aims to set out on the right foot in order to arrive at a successful conclusion. There is, however, a major difference between the end of a game of chess and the end of (or exit from) an analysis. The endgame in chess means that there are no further moves to be made, but an analysis, progressing via interpretations, usually ends for an analysand with a range of pulsations and movements.

An interpretation is supposed to impact repetition, bringing it to a halt. But what, really, is repetition in analysis and why is it manifested in analytic work? Many analysands go to an analyst in order to find an ally who will help them to challenge a repetitive pattern, which they have already identified. They are exasperated or feel cornered by a dysfunctional pattern, but have no idea how to break out of it. Conversely, there are cases where the patient is either unaware of the pattern or gains so much enjoyment from the repetition that they are not really ready or willing to let go of it. Beneath any analytic interpretation, there is the question posed to the analysand: 'Do you really want to know?'. When exactly is this question posed to the analysand?

As Lacan reminds us early on in his *Seminar* (Lacan, 1953–4), the analyst's intervention/interpretation cuts across everyday 'bla bla' in order to create a space where truth can be spoken, regardless of how painful it might be for a subject to confront this space. By targeting repetition such an intervention is targeting a crucial aspect of the drive.

Coming back to the analogy between that first move in a game of chess and analytic interpretation: an interpretation can be contingent (Lacan uses the Greek word, 'tuché'), like the opening move that the chess player chooses from among many alternatives, none of which are obviously better than the others, and yet the interpretation and the chess move can be hugely influential for what happens later (in the treatment and in the game). It is not so much the mode of interpretation, its content or how it is formulated or expressed, which is most important, but rather what is targeted at a precise moment. That moment can then be transformed into a momentum, creating a dynamism in the work. Or, it can unblock a journey that goes beyond previously held assumptions. This theory of interpretation was Lacan's response to the analytic resistances that were encountered when the first generation of psychoanalysts trapped themselves in a web of fixed meanings, which made it harder to do justice to clinical material. The Lacanian approach saw a shock value in the very act of interpretation, associated with the position of the analyst, which is not to say that shock should be an end in itself, but that interpretation – by reversing the analysand's discourse in such a way that he or she hears what they are trying so hard to hide from themselves – generates an effect of shock.

This can be a painful process. Such intervention dares the analysand to approach a type of knowledge that has a meaning only for the subject – a knowledge about their desire or symptom or something about their drive organisation. Transference acts as an ally to interpretation (the interpretation will only be sanctioned and have an effect if transference is in place). In his *Seminar XI*, Lacan refers to interpretation in analysis as a signification unlike any other signification. He tells us (referring to a case extract put forward for discussion by Serge Leclaire) that an interpretation is directed towards a nonsensical meaning. In other words, an interpretation should target a signifier in a subject's narrative which is not reducible to any meaning. It is the *effect* of an interpretation at the level of the signifier (not the signified), which counts as an analytic act. Lacan elaborates that such an interpretation is 'essential to the advent of the subject' (Lacan, 1963–4, p. 250). The signifier that is targeted is the one, to which the subject is subjected and which the subject expresses in the narrative of his or her life events but without lending it anything like the meaning that is evoked by the interpretation. Lacan reminds us of Freud's 'Wolfman' case history and asserts that 'wolf' is the 'originally repressed signifier' which is 'nonsensical' (Lacan, 1963–4, p. 251). What does this mean and how does this particular signifier appear in the clinic of psychoanalysis?

A clinical vignette might be helpful. An analysand suffering from anxiety attacks comes to sessions and brings dreams that often contain the word 'sea'. She is considering whether to have children with her partner. Her prospective maternity (her feminine position) leads her to explore and elaborate her relationship with her own mother. The relationship has been challenging, but she insists on involving her mother in her life, particularly as she contemplates becoming a mother herself. Her dreams of 'sea' occurred in gaps when she and her mother did not speak, usually after a dispute or quarrel. In one session, she asked if she could sit on the chair facing the analyst instead of lying on the couch. This was agreed. On her way out of the session, the analyst asked whether she would be willing to continue on the couch. She replied unwillingly: 'Let's see …' The analyst drew her attention the homophony between 'see' and 'sea'. The effect was surprising. In the next session, the analysand was struck for the first time by her own insistence on her mother's presence and involvement in her life. She linked it specifically to her mother's gaze (by which her mother *sees* her). Despite all the criticism which she levelled against her mother, the analysand was seeking her approval. It emerged later in the work how the maternal gaze has been substituted in the analysand's life by the gaze of other significant people. Her anxiety became acute whenever she came too close to being the ideal girl for her mother. To become her (the mother) was her desire as a woman. But what was 'her' for this analysand? It was *the woman*! In this clinical example, the signifier 'sea/see' did not have any particular meaning that the analytic interpretation singled out. It was ubiquitous, but, like a ghost, it had no material weight in the domain of meanings. An element in the circuit of the scopic drive was targeted in the subject's narrative in a way that was made possible by the transference. The analysand was engaged in the work and willing to use the interpretation because of love and trust experienced at the level of transference. Otherwise, the analyst's intervention would have fallen on deaf ears.

Early in life there can be a narrative, which is significant: an interpretation has already been made, on the basis of which a subject comes into being. In other words, a sense/meaning of the subject's being for the Other (signification) is constituted after an equivocal narrative in the mother tongue is heard and misrecognised/misinterpreted. The original meaning of the Other's narrative is challenged when it is subjectively interpreted. Each subject forms the core of their symptom in a certain way, following their own interpretation of something said by the caregiver (Morel, 2019). In analysis, we go backwards to this earlier construction of signification. The direction of the analytic work, led by interpretation, enables the subject's knot of being to unravel in order to be rewoven in accordance with their desire. Such an unravelling depends on effective interpretation. The shock that comes after certain 'Aha!' moments in analysis is the motor that sustains the analysand's desire to know or to make new knowledge out of that, which determines the subject's being.

Lacanians have a reputation for doing analysis in an eccentric manner: giving short and variable-length sessions, treating money (the fee of the sessions) as an intervention on the unconscious material, using silence or theatrical interpretations in the clinic, neither interpreting transference nor attempting to induce transference and using shock tactics to create dynamism in the unconscious. Preference for 'oracular' or equivocal interpretations instead of a well-polished, meaningful mini-lecture at the end of each session has created a myth of Lacanian psychoanalysis being useful only for intellectuals, but too 'difficult' for most. The truth, though, is that the Lacanian approach is not loveless, abstract or meaningless, as these criticisms would imply. Lacanian interpretation targets the 'alien' knowledge of the subject of the unconscious – knowledge which it takes courage to face. Emphasis on this most alien knowledge, which is the truth of a subject marked by sexuality, mortality and the law of language, complicates the mode of practice of the practitioner. A certain 'cowardice', which Lacan pointed out towards the end of his work, is an effect related to this alienating knowledge: an attitude of 'I don't want to know' towards such anguish-provoking knowledge makes the journey of analysis complicated. Many people need time before they are ready to hear what they have hitherto refused to hear. Also, many analysands are loathe to surrender an addiction to 'received' knowledge and to endure not knowing. The knowledge that is sought is not a universal cause of clinical conditions, but rather something specific to the formation of each analysand's symptom. To go against understanding is challenging and the long journey of analysis is evidence of the complications that come with our status as speaking beings. Interpretation points at something beyond the immediate grasp of a subject who is ruled by the rational and intellectual, and the notion of Lacanian analysis as an intellectual journey is not only absurd but contrary to how the orientation works. Psychoanalysis, in the Lacanian approach, is a long process where interpretation has a navigating function, pointing towards nothingness.

The shock value of an interpretation, which Lacan emphasised, is not about surprising the analysand by the acuteness of the analyst's intuition; it targets the determined, although unconscious resistance of the subject to knowing about the enjoyment of his or her being. The impact of such an interpretation is manifested as surprise, which might be expressed by the words 'You've got me!' The subject now faces a choice between bad and worse – whether to give up on a mode of enjoyment and endorse a loss (bad) or to shrug off the knowledge and persist in the enjoyment (worse, at least from the point of view of the analysis). In the limited window of choice that each of us has, as a mortal and social being, we might respond with defiance, a bungled action or an acting out, each of which could express one or other of these choices, or (more likely) a mixture of the two.

How does analysis really work? is an enigma which both intrigues and hinders a subject from searching for the truth of their being. An interpretation can, therefore, help the analysand in their endeavour to go beyond the ordinary way of understanding, but can also cause despair and frustration – a sense that much hard work towards conscious understanding (to reach a safe place where they can leave the impossible-to-know in peace) has been cancelled out.

Lacanians are well known for using equivocal interpretation. Such interpretations can be at the level of homophony, logic or grammar. For instance, an analysand might say, 'Is he my husband?', and the analyst, to highlight a mode of feminine jouissance might reply, 'Are you his wife?' Or a homophonic play on *tuer* and *tu es* (in French, respectively, 'to kill' and 'you are') may be used as an interpretation to pinpoint an underlying rage or death wish. An analysand once remarked to the analyst, 'It is not me telling you this,' to which the analyst replied, 'Another person is not telling me this!'

One might ask, 'why do we treat an analysand's narrative like this?' According to Lacan, the significance of our being originates from a subjective interpretation. This initial interpretation which can form the core of our symptom is usually an interpretation of an enigmatic or equivocal narrative originating from a caregiver. In analysis the direction is reversed in order to get closer to the core of the enjoyment that is obtained from a symptom: with the help of equivocal interpretation, we move away from or deconstruct what has been constructed around the meaning and value of our being for the Other, in order to get back to the earliest narrative from which we wove our being. Why is this useful? The clinic of psychoanalysis shows us that a subject comes to an analyst when they are cornered by the impossibility of enjoying, usually after they have recognised a series of destructive repetitive patterns. Through the journey of analysis, after much exploration of past events, an access to their preferred way of enjoying their life can be gained when they recognise the extent to which the fundamental meaning of being echoed in their desire and symptom is dependent on the Other. The excitement of life at the level of the drive can then become more available to the subject. They might also realise that certain foundational narratives of their significant Other do not matter anymore. An analytic interpretation facilitates such fundamental adjustment to the significance of being. A new meaning and significance for one's being can be constructed again at that point, generating a mode of enjoyment and freedom to enjoy and appreciate one's life (this is usually the principal challenge in the clinic of obsessional neurosis).

The trajectory of analysis goes from self-presentation in a 'personal statement' to gradually allowing oneself to be articulated in gaps that take one unawares and generate surprise. When a narrative around a painful state of being is presented in analysis (anxiety attack, low mood, insomnia, sexual dysfunction, etc.), an analyst pays attention to how the narrative is uttered and the logic or argument though which it is brought to analysis, and does so prior to making any assumptions, interpretations or interventions. The analyst's mode of listening is attuned to identifying what is not said, heard or noticed and, more importantly, to why this is so.

Let us take an example to clarify this. A young man comes to analysis when his partner leaves him. In the first meeting, he focuses on his intolerable anxiety and is determined to find what it was that caused the breakup. He says, perplexed, 'But we were a perfect couple!' and continues, 'Clearly not! we ended up becoming estranged from one another'. As mentioned earlier, there are a hundred ways to intervene on such statements, but there is usually one way which challenges the subjective construction of the analysand's being. The analytic interpretation aims to indicate a path which will go via exploration and elaboration of the constructions and understandings that the subject has fabricated. The young man's first statement starts with a 'but', a word that indicates a contrast. One way to enter the maze is to wonder if there was another way in which he and his girlfriend were together, a way that was less perfect. The analyst says!, 'You were…, but a perfect couple!' What sort of couple they had been up until that point might say much about what Lacan calls 'the sexual non-rapport'. It could identify the analysand's symptom and mode of enjoyment or perhaps his inability to allow himself to enjoy life. Exploration of the vague expression 'perfect' could also be a fruitful opening for analytic work. The impossibility for the subject to see what seemed obvious to others in his love relationship was formulated and posed to him as a piece of the puzzle. When the work unfolded and developed towards an extensive elaboration of earlier events in his life, what emerged was a hatred towards his father who was blamed for his failings not as a father but as a husband. And yet, as he realised in the course of the work, he had taken up a similar position to his father in his own relationship. Where to proceed from there? He spent a few sessions considering the possibilities. At this stage in the work, he criticised his father for being selfish and putting himself before anyone else in the family. 'My father wanted to be satisfied at all costs'. 'At all costs?', the analyst asked. 'Yes, to be happy at the cost of the unhappiness of others'. He explained that happy (another vague signifier) was interpreted by him as 'easily satisfied'. 'And what is the opposite of being easily satisfied?', the analyst asks. 'Being better, being great', he replied. 'And how badly do you want to be great?' The analyst paused the session there.

His father's stance towards his mode of enjoyment (his ethical stance) had found an expression in the subject's guilt or inability to allow himself enjoyment, and this had left its mark on his relationship with his ex-partner. His own symptom of 'becoming great' or perhaps 'greater than his father' was highlighted through the aforementioned interventions. And so the work began.

In this book we explore how analytic interpretation actually works. Rather than taking a purely conceptual approach, the contributors, who are all themselves practising analysts, describe moments at which something changed for them when they were in the role of analysand in their own personal analysis. Insights, revelations, connections, meanings and non-meanings all feature in these accounts of crucial moments in analysis and give the reader a sense of what the process is all about. Coming from a broad range of analysts – some with years of experience and others just starting out – these vignettes will hopefully show how change takes place and will be of interest and value to anyone curious about the analytic process.

The vignettes are from the field of Lacanian analysis and will hopefully counter clichéd views of what Lacanians actually do in their work. The examples of interpretation and its effects extend from what seems very classical to what seems radically innovative, showing the use of humour, theatre and the body in psychoanalytic practice. Personal testimony on the question of interpretation comes from the personal analysis of each contributor, and each vignette is published anonymously. Since we aim to make this book accessible to readers outside psychoanalytic circles, we have avoided using psychoanalytic jargon as much as possible.

So far as we know, no book in English about Lacanian analysis has attempted to do anything comparable, and we hope to address a broad range of readers, since the topic is relevant both to workers in the field and to anyone who has considered embarking on a talking therapy. As each section will be brief (sometimes as brief as a couple of sentences), readers can tune in and out as they please, giving the book a different feel to other publications about analytic interpretation. The huge variety of vignettes will show the reader how diverse analytic practice is, dispelling stereotyped views about how interpretation works and what forms it takes.

We hope that the volume will do things a little differently from the plethora of works that attempt to explain how analysis works (or should work). Dogmatic views on the nature of analysis deserve to be challenged, and more discussion of the nature of the knowledge at stake in analytic discourse is needed.

Berjanet Jazani
London, Autumn 2023

Bibliography

Freud, S. (1899). Interpretation of Dreams. In: J. Strachey, ed. *The Standard Edition of the Complete Psychological Works of Sigmund Freud*, Vol 4. London: Vintage, 2001, 1–631.

Freud, S. (1913). On Beginning the Treatment. PP. 121–145. In: J. Strachey, ed. *The Standard Edition of the Complete Psychological Works of Sigmund Freud*, Vol 12. London: Vintage, 2001.

Lacan, J. (1953–4). *The Seminar of Jacques Lacan: BookI: Freud's Papers on Technique*. John Forrester (Trans). Norton. New York & London.

Lacan, J. (1963–4). *The seminar of Jacques Lacan: Book XI: The Four Fundamental Concepts of Psychoanalysis*. Alan Sheridan (Trans). New York & London: Norton.

Morel, G. (2019). *The Law of the Mother: An Essay on the Sexual Sinthome*. Lindsay Watson (Trans.). London: Routledge.

A Question That Put Me to Work

During my first analysis in the 1980s, there was a week when strike actions simultaneously affected all means of public transport. There were no buses, tubes or trains, and roads were gridlocked with cars. Three times a week I went for sessions, travelling on public transport from my place of work in south London to north London where my analyst practiced. As I had no other access to transport, I decided that I would leave work earlier and walk to my session. I build up quite a sweat during the nearly two-hour walk but made it just in time for the session. I proudly told my analyst that I had walked almost ten miles in record pace to get to my session on time. Rather than congratulating me on what I considered to be a heroic effort demonstrating my keen commitment to my analysis, she retorted 'Why did you do that?' I felt immensely disappointed and deflated by this question which I had little desire to explore. However, this moment and the intervention of the analyst aiming right at what I was trying to be for the (m)other proved something of a turning point and has resonated many times over the years. It was a question that touched squarely on my subjective implication and phantasmatic construction. It took me a long time to hear that in my analyst's question – 'Why did you do that?' – a margin of subjective freedom was also indicated.

DOI: 10.4324/9781032637723-1

110

A decade after the end of my first analysis, while trying to work through a new blossoming of an old symptom, I consulted a second analyst.

After the first session, I realised that I had not asked about the fee, and nor had the analyst brought it up. I was surprised that I hadn't said anything, given my apparent curiosity about what the figure might be (I wanted to work two or more times a week, would I be able to afford it, could I justify it, etc.).

As soon as the second session ended, I realised, again, that there had been no mention of money. I felt a little anxious and entered the third session determined to ask at the very beginning. Face to face with the analyst, however, my question vanished. This third meeting started with my father, as I'd said at the end of the previous session that one of the effects of my first analysis was that I had finally been able to mourn his sudden death many years earlier. I repeated a well-worn phrase that I had used often over the years, having just changed the respective ages as time passed:

> "My father would have been 100 now and his first wife would have been 110." I added that she had left behind not only my father but their three sons, 13, 11 and 10 at the time of her death.

The analyst asked about my own mother, my father's second wife. I said that she was 83, 17 years younger than my father, and that they met when my mother was a newly qualified nurse of 23 and my father a recently widowed 40. He was one of her first patients, admitted to hospital in the overwhelming and whisky-laden wake of death.

At the start of session four, I blurted out my question and said something about how anxious I'd been about it. There was no immediate, direct reply, but instead a request for me to speak about my mother's grandparents. While the taking of a wide and detailed history is not unusual at the start of a Lacanian analysis, it surprised me in its specificity, and I was pleased to speak about them.

DOI: 10.4324/9781032637723-2

After a pause, the analyst asked:

"So, can you pay 110 a session?"
"Oh god", I thought, "that's a lot." "Yes", I replied, "I can."
The analyst ended the session.

My father's first wife had long been an object of fascination for me, but until the "110" moment I don't think I'd realised quite how much. I'd heard of her striking auburn hair, her proficiency at poker and on horseback, her wit and her "strong character." I liked her unusual and interesting name. I had even romanticised the facts of and around her death, particularly the narrative of my father having "nursed" her for the last two years of her life.

What was the analyst aiming at when they suggested "110"? It may have been their standard fee of course (if they had such a thing), but I don't think that was the case. In pointing me straight back towards the signifier 110, the analyst highlighted my preoccupation with this dead woman and her relationship to my father, a preoccupation that obscured my parents and their relationship, one without which I would not exist. The presence of this woman, like the fee, had seemed "a lot." And the sudden swerve to the analyst's interest in my mother's grandparents, at that particular moment, opened something up.

In Seminar XI, Lacan said what is essential in a significant interpretation is that the analysand "should see, beyond this signification, to what signifier – to what irreducible, traumatic, non-meaning – he is, as a subject, subjected."

The underlining of the 110 jolted me into seeing something of what I had allowed myself to be subjected to. It led to an ongoing engagement with and writing of my own family history, no longer barred by this once-fascinating object.

Some months ago my mother died, and while writing this piece, I thought about how I would now respond if I had reason to say something about my parents. Changing the respective ages as time passes, this would simply be:

My father would have been 102 now and my mother would have been 85.

My Teddy Collection

My analysis began when I was 16 years of age. I was having a difficult relationship with my mother, and she thought I should speak to someone. I was angry and rebellious, but I didn't understand why. I was starting to embark on a path of self-destruction, and I truly believe psychoanalysis saved me. I began to understand there were unconscious reasons why I felt the way I did and why I behaved the way I did. Transference had the power to ground me, and I felt I had a safe place to speak, where I could be heard. My analyst was interested in my feelings and this was a novelty for me.

It was through the narration of my life story that I started to connect the dots and interpret my symptoms with the aid of my analyst's careful listening, her punctuations and her remarks. It was a relief to speak freely, without fear of judgement, and there was a sense that my analyst would not dislike me if I showed her my flaws. She only cared about my side of the story, and this is what is so unique about the strange relationship one forms with one's analyst. When people say they can speak to friends and family about anything, well, sometimes it is difficult to address issues you have with them, and we often disregard the fact that they have their own feelings in relation to us which will influence the kind of advice and support they can give.

So, I had to figure out why was my mother so triggering for me? What had she done to make me so angry and impatient with her? It was strange because so far I had only idealised her. In analysis I heard myself speak about abandonment and neglect, all that had been repressed, feelings that had not even been named. The resentment had been masked by my mother's beauty and her status of semi-celebrity, because being her daughter meant I was like her, or at least, I came from her, so how can I despise her and miss out on my 'kudos' by association?

After some time in analysis, I realised I was angry because my mother was trying to enforce her authority over me, a respect she had not earned! She is my biological mother, but for me being a mother means raising a child, not abandoning a child in the hands of your family, living and working abroad, and then returning to claim your status. As a child I felt my mother fooled me: her love came in the form of a suitcase full of gifts – there was always a cute teddy she brought from Disney World or Japan.

DOI: 10.4324/9781032637723-3

At this point in my life, now aged 19, I was suffering terribly from any small rejection in my love life, and I coped with this by replacing boys in a series, one after another. I will never forget a session in which I was telling my analyst about the latest romance and how that was going and how I had been suffering from the previous guy…when she intervened by asking me: 'So when are you going to stop collecting cuddly toys?' She cut the session. I laughed nervously. The interpretation resonated. I was trying to find in a partner what my mother couldn't give me. Yet I was repeating a pattern by going for people who would reject me. I was the fool believing that cute boy-teddies were going to fill the void. I wanted to stop the collection, and the analysis helped me formulate my problem: I wasn't sure I was lovable yet I demanded nothing but love from the other.

Playing Games

I do not lie on a couch. I sit in a chair and have done so for four years but only for the last two with a Lacanian analyst. For roughly 45 minutes – never much more or less – I sit, sometimes speaking, sometimes silent. The invitation is to say anything, but often it is difficult to say even something. I find myself here twice weekly because of a symptom that has intruded daily for 25 years – a symptom that conscripts the body, stealing hours of each day, owning me for that time and then leaking into everything else. Impossible to bear in the end, sutured to a shameful pleasure that sustains it nonetheless. The decision to consult an analyst is driven by this, inspired by this daily repetition – a repetition in action, an insistent disruption to the flow of my life, a disturbance in how I think about myself.

In these last few years, with the opportunity to say things out loud to someone who listens closely and says little, but is by no means silent, I have come to understand many things about why I find myself here, trapped in this relentless cycle. I can trace back many of the footprints of the unconscious that have marked me, the origins and meanings of the closed circuit that confines me. I think I see the part I play in my own suffering. I see how the not-saying of things keeps me stuck and I try to say more. Nothing much changes though. Still, I turn up to sessions religiously. I read insistently, compulsively looking for answers, hungry to know more, urgently trying to better understand – as if that holds the key.

Then, just over a year into my current analysis, I have a distinctive session one summer afternoon. This does not provoke anything close to a personal transformation, yet some part of something important does change. It is a rather simple, unexceptional moment, and it is difficult to say much about the how and why of its effect, but afterwards things are different. The symptom miraculously attenuates into a much milder version of the same beast, freeing up hours of my day though still clinging on tightly in morphed form so that I can be in no doubt there are still many words left to be said, many hours still to be sat, many silences still to be borne.

In any case, I leave this one particular session feeling terrible about myself. But it is not that feeling, that seems to have an effect but, rather, it is its accompanying shock value that reverberates. It is its unexpectedness and foreignness that leaves a mark. After all, I have felt terrible about myself on numerous occasions before.

DOI: 10.4324/9781032637723-4

This is different, unexpectedly jolting. What then of this jolting moment, and its before and after?

Brought up in a family where all interactions were mediated through sports and games – through keeping a score, through challenges and rematch requests, through tallies and points – it is not until my analyst takes the idea of 'playing games' out of the familial, sporting context in which I have often spoken of it and sits it alongside my symptom that I abruptly see myself in a different light. An unfamiliar light tinged with a competitive edge that extends beyond the sporting field, where I recognise it, and into a more general way of operating, where I do not. Until this moment that is.

However obvious in retrospect, it is only thanks to the 'slap in the face' of this recontextualisation that I grasp that, when it comes to my symptom, I want to be better at it than anyone else – and I think I am. I imagine that I exercise it with more frequency, and with greater ease, with greater secrecy and to greater effect than anyone else. I am convinced of this. I am the best at it. The bars perhaps one other close competitor. I find myself wondering whether, rather than being gripped by my symptom, I might be the one keeping a very tight grip on it – and onto other things too. Something gets reframed by that reversal. I feel like a stranger to myself, unrecognisably recognisable.

In the fallout from that moment, and for the following six months, the symptom dilutes remarkably. But not beyond that, the change is short-lived. There is no transformation to speak of, more of a false start at best. The unsustainability of the change, coupled with the redoubled force of the symptom, prompts a despairing panic linked to a new question – how to loosen this paralysing grip, how to extricate from this contest and disentangle from this dear competitor who, ironically, has been complained of at such length over the years. Speaking in sessions becomes harder than ever. I wonder to what degree I am determined to keep playing the same game ad infinitum, sustaining this wretched and perversely gratifying status quo. I find myself right back where I started, only in a completely different place.

Queer Dead Uncles

Interpretation emerges belatedly. The sessions themselves, and the pauses between them, are filled with little tools that might eventually amount to an interpretative scaffolding: descriptions (of events), articulations (of feelings), and unexpected associations (between events and feelings). Sometimes I cheat and come up with connections before the session begins so that I am a bit more armed when it does. If I remember a dream and write it down, I feel less naked for analysis, too. Ready to offer the analyst something that isn't just silence, from which anything can emerge. So many decades into analysis (I began as a teenager), I may still not be ready for this "anything" that can emerge. I may rehearse the topic ahead of time, but when the session starts, all bets are off. Perhaps "anything" won't emerge, but certainly something that wasn't accounted for.

Interpretation is never settled, then. It is made of working hypotheses that roam in the scene of analysis. At times, an interpretation seems convincing only because it provides a structure. A few sessions later, it feels a little too neat for it to be true. The scaffolding loses strength. Like in a film, where a discrete but recurring element announces itself as particularly meaningful and begs to be deciphered. That element can always turn out to be a red herring. Holding on to it without the benefit of time, without reconsidering the validity of its relevance a million times, can be dangerous. How to tell interpretation apart from an interpretative fantasy?

I trust more interpretations that are crafted little by little and take the shape of disarming questions more so than explanations. There are destabilizing questions, questions that allow one to move, to loosen up the stitches that hold our parts together under false pretences. Because to arrive in analysis is to have as one's body the sedimentation of a host of age-old, if not ancestral, interpretations that analysis must debunk—or, at least, interrogate. This is what analysis does: it dissolves interpretations we have inherited, or sewn together like a carapace, in order to make room for the unaccounted for to emerge.

The raw material for these long-lasting and ever-shifting interpretations is an accumulation of insights, motifs, or repetitions made conscious when I catch myself saying something I had never considered and whose clarity stuns me or when the analyst marks something as fertile, or fundamental, by repeating a word that came

DOI: 10.4324/9781032637723-5

out of my mouth or when she suggests a (new) direction in thinking by cutting the session short: "We'll stop here."

Interpretation isn't something that dawns on me. Although it may take shape as speculations conjured in a session, or between sessions, interpretation follows the painstaking logic of sewing, or writing; that is, interpretation is a practice. It is an incessant compositing. It is revisiting and reworking, experimenting with new cuts and angles, adding new layers, stretching them out to see if they break—one at a time. In the end, there is no map or linear narrative to read, no authentication from the analyst, but a kind of tissue that I can wear and see if it fits. A key part of seeing if something fits is being able to take it off.

One of the most consequential of these bric-a-brac mantles that I have managed to fashion in analysis brings together my earliest and my most recent insights regarding what I have come to call my queer dead uncles. I have two uncles who died very young before I was born, one on each side, mother and father. They have gained a queer quality by virtue of being dead, by virtue of being ghostly, and by virtue of being dissidents. One was in love with philosophy and literature. He drowned at the age of 17. The other was part of the struggle against the Brazilian dictatorship, killed in a car accident in his early 20s on his way to vote. The first was always locked in his bedroom, reading Sartre, or Kafka. The other was always described as a Jesus-like hero of the resistance against bourgeois viciousness, against good manners, and against frivolity: a paragon of ethical behaviour and activism. These were odd men, queer in their refusal to coincide with the mediocrity of their times, of their peers, queer in their commitment to politics and art, queer in the tenderness of their demeanour. To be a man and to not thrive in violence was, in their environment and in mine, to be queer, to be dead.

Little by little I came to the realization, or speculation, that I had forged my own demeanour, my tastes, ambitions, and orientations, in an attempt to pick up where these queer dead uncles left off. They had architected me as I grew up sandwiched between them, incestuously, certain that in my family to be queer was to die too soon. Except that given the fact that my existence took shape decades after theirs had ended, I was able to exercise my queerness in much more literal ways, ways that flirted with trans-ness, both of which seemed, in any case, always already aimed at death too. And I wouldn't even have to drown, or get into a car accident, to achieve the lethal climax of my queerness. All I had to do was simply live it—queerness—and AIDS would take care of it in due time. Of that I was sure at age 9 or earlier. In fact, this was my childhood's most profound certainty: I am queer, and I will die of AIDS, whether I ever kiss another boy or not. This is my inheritance.

Through analysis, I slowly developed the notion that I had attempted to incarnate my parents' dead brothers in order to guarantee their love. As such, the queer dead uncles provided a compass, although not evenly, for despite their similarities, these uncles are not the same. I had tried to be a certified copy of my mother's brother mostly, the one who drowned, the one who read, and the one who locked himself in the bedroom with my mother to recite poetry to her—the only 2 beings in a home of 14 people who cared about books, who owned books, and who loved books. The decisions I made for my career, where books are not only crucial but the kind of books the drowned uncle, would have likely gravitated towards, and the way my tastes developed, pointed to this act of impersonation, or reparation, or the facilitation of a mourning, particularly in relationship to my mother and her lack that hurt the most: a brother. My father's dead brother too haunted me into a position, particularly in regard to his unwavering investment in ethical principles, uncannily captured by the portrait of Che Guevara that hung above my little bed since I was a baby, with the words, "Hay que endurecerse sin perder jamás la ternura" ("One must endure without ever losing tenderness") across the bottom.

Interpretation is always unfinished. Because it is a working hypothesis, I sense it can be proven wrong at any moment, exposed as wishful thinking, or evolve into a much more complex and perhaps, more enlightening operation. This is what happened in my most recent interpretative episodes in analysis, where the proverbial other shoe finally dropped. It occurred to me that, indeed, these physically absent uncles had taken up so much room in my psychic life, and in my analytical sessions, from the beginning, or even before it, but I had always also had an aunt—and one that was physically present in all the stages of my life. This aunt, Lena, who is only a year younger than my mother, was perhaps the only adult in my life, growing up as a child in a brutally queerphobic atmosphere, for whom my queerness would not have been a problem. My aunt, who travelled hundreds of miles to attend my every birthday, who let me stay up until the wee hours watching movies for grown-ups, who bought me ice cream and expensive shirts, who cuddled me when my mother spanked me, who listened when I put my hatred for my father into words as a ten-year-old, who put her personal life on hold to fly to Mexico to babysit me for months when I was two years old. My aunt, the only person in my extended family whose hair colour was the same as mine, the only one to ever cloak me with laughter and openness and glee. My aunt, the only person I had ever seen say something nice about gay men until the age of 17. The only one who dared to speak of homophobia, not of homosexuals, without disdain and mockery. The one who never married, the one who told her nieces to masturbate because it wasn't wrong, the one who listened to Madonna with me at 11 and tried to learn the choreography, why was she not in my dreams?

Why was she not in my sessions? Why was she not the ghostly hand whipping me into shape? My aunt, the queerest of them all!

At last, an interpretation that provides an opening, not a story. A disturbing set of questions, not resolutions. Finally, an inheritance that is actually alive.

Today it is the aunt I try to turn to. The aunt I did have, not the uncles I didn't. The aunt who when asked why I am obsessed with Madonna to this day, doesn't dismiss my desire as infantile faggotry, but offers lucidity and light: "Because you wanted to be her."

La Cough

As the story goes, Lacan's most infamous intervention did not employ a signifier, phoneme, or cut, but rather a movement of his body. In the documentary "Rendezvous Chez Lacan", his patient who had lived through the Nazi occupation of France as a child explains that she continues to wake up in panic at 5am each morning. This was the hour that the Gestapo would search the homes. At that point, Lacan jumps out of his chair, crosses the room, and gently caresses her cheek. For her, the intervention transformed the foreboding signifier Gestapo into a tender gesture: "geste à peau". This was a transformative moment in the patient's "talking cure" that involved no talking on the part of the analyst, only attention and a spontaneous movement.

When I was just beginning my practice as analyst, through some distortion in my reading of Freud (or Freudians), I concocted the fantasy that the analyst should be silent and still, rigorously methodical, and only intervene with thoroughly premeditated, theoretically sound interpretations. In other words, the analyst should be dead. This ideal paralyzed me in practice as I was trapped in the misconception that I wasn't supposed to have a body, breathe, or be human. Following hours of listening to analysands in a state of anxious paralysis, I questioned how this work of psychoanalysis, pulsing with the life of the body in theory (oral, anal, phallus, jouissance), could become so frozen in practice.

I believe that much of this congealed ideal was the product of my own experience in analysis with a contemporary Freudian, whom I thank in retrospect for encouraging my movement towards starting a new analysis with a particular Lacanian. I had become charmed by this analyst while attending her seminar. A few sessions into the new analysis, I was lying on the couch, stiff and anxious, trying my best to "free associate" in the presence of the woman I so admired. Then, I heard a faint gurgle, followed by a cough, some rummaging around, and a few gulps. I didn't dare turn my head to verify events, but the sounds that touched my ears evinced the presence of an imperfect human body. In response, my body eased and my speech began to flow. It was then that the analysis could begin.

Of course, this accidental nonintervention occurred against the backdrop of my trust in her as an analyst, knowing her years of experience and investment in Lacan. I had been so enthralled by her seminar that when I first encountered her in

DOI: 10.4324/9781032637723-6

the treatment room, she was not just the "subject supposed to know" (a belief that drives an analysis) but the subject who actually did know. In the face of imagined complete knowledge, speech felt not only impossible but unnecessary. Something needed to be lacking. Her body blunder poked a hole in her perfection, opening a gap in which I could speak.

I draw the link between my analyst's gurgle cough and Lacan's "geste à peau" because both "interventions" fall outside of psychoanalytic convention by engaging primarily the body of the analyst. In both cases, their effect rested on a myriad of contingencies to coincide with what would work for the patient at a particular moment. The success of Lacan's tender gesture hinged on the patient's ability to use it to transform the signifier, and hence its impact on her body. My analyst's brief failing was the nudge I needed to be able not only to begin my own analysis but to become a suspiring, imperfect analyst myself.

Motherhood

Lying next to my nine-month-old as she sleeps, I realise there are so many moments where I've felt something has shifted for me in analysis. And it feels apt to write about a moment of revelation regarding my new position as a mother, making space for myself and within my relationships, as I am unable to get up without waking the baby and have very little time to myself.

I came to my analyst with a sadness and frustration over a set of decisions that needed to be made, decisions involving childcare arrangements, work commitments and buying a house, and I had given myself an unnecessarily short timescale to make them.

All these decisions affected one another and I felt frozen, not knowing where to start, and panicked to make them all at once, which was causing tensions in my relationship.

I love my daughter more than anything and I love caring for her. And for the first time I have had to completely put any development of my personal career on hold, for an uncertain period of time as we all adjust to life as a family.

After expressing these worries in the first of two sessions that afternoon, my analyst asked me the question: 'So what is the problem?'

I was surprised, as I thought that I had spent the last 20 minutes talking about the problem!

The pause in the session allowed me at that point to reflect on my speech, the words I was using, what was at stake, what would I lose if these decisions were not made, conversations not had, now.

During this pause, I realised that an overarching fear I had was the fear of the continued loss of my identity before having a baby. Not knowing the answers to these decisions meant not having a date in the future which would symbolise for me the 're starting' of my self, myself beyond being a mother.

The fear of not knowing was eclipsing the present, casting a shadow over becoming a mother.

The question posed to me at that point in my analysis gave me the space to allow these fears to rise to the surface, beyond the demands of practical decision-making. To search in-between the words to find a deeper cause of frustration, to look at something that had been just beyond my recognition for months – that in

DOI: 10.4324/9781032637723-7

struggling to hold onto something that was gone, I wasn't letting myself become something new.

Realising this took the pressure off making these decisions.

During the second session, in voicing this to my analyst – and to myself – I drew on a memory from childhood, which had up until this point only been connected in my mind to time spent in Australia as a child.

A life guard visited our class to discuss safety on the beach. If you ever got taken out to sea by a riptide, you were advised not to struggle against it, wearing yourself out. Instead, let the rip take you out, try to stay calm and keep afloat, and eventually the rip would bring you back to shore, further down the coast.

In trying to explain my fears of loss of self in analysis, I was a person caught in a rip tide, struggling to return to a shore I would never be able to return to, one where I did not have a child.

By struggling, I was not accepting my position becoming a mother and as an individual who would never be the same again.

By struggling, I was not allowing myself to be drawn away and towards another shore, one where I was a mother and an individual, but changed forever because of the process of having a child.

To let myself be where I was in this current moment, I needed to trust I would find myself again.

By accepting the not knowing, I would make space to discover who I would become as an individual and a better mother for my daughter, than if I were fighting to return to something that was gone.

I also began to recognise that I was identifying with my own mother, who had children at a young age and was unable to dedicate time to herself as a parent in her early twenties. My panic and sense of urgency took on a more significant meaning beyond my personal situation as I reflected on the similarities between her past behaviours and mine at this time. Were my feelings related more strongly to my mother's story in the past than my own?

The ambiguity of 'What is the problem?' allowed me to follow a line of enquiry in my mind without dismissing certain thoughts that came up along the way – thoughts I may have disregarded if the question asked at that moment was specifically aimed at the practical issues I initially brought to the session.

The scope of the question allowed space for me to face something that up until that point I had been unable to face.

There was space for me to talk around the point, and I came to realise my deeper fears and make valuable connections and separations between my story and my mother's story through my own interpretation and in my own way. This gave me agency and confidence to accept a loss and begin to embrace the metamorphosis of becoming a mother.

The image of the sea that came to me during this session is one that now reminds me to trust myself and to embrace who I am becoming during moments of frustration, a frustration that may not even be mine but an inherited one. Perhaps in another set of circumstances, or if the question had not been asked, I may never have seen what was hiding in plain sight.

Why Hypothesize?

Early on in my analysis, I learned the importance of searching for unknown knowns, those fragments of thoughts, affects, sentences, and narratives that had fallen off the beaten path, rolled off my default mode network, but lay breathing in a land beyond my ego. Stumbling across these powerful fragments was rare. It often required a certain mood, a patience, and a creative quantum of space within my analysis. But sometimes, all it needed was a hypothesis.

My analyst rarely said much. However, a few months into my analysis, when I was questioning the validity of a bipolar diagnosis I had been given many years ago, he asked me for my personal theory, my hypothesis for my shifting moods. It was an interesting question, perhaps a distant, more forgiving cousin of the more aggressive, highly demanding "Why?" "Why?" is a tough question that is easily avoided, a question that reveals either known knowns or known unknowns. "Why?" is very much a neighbourhood within my default mode network. A hypothesis, on the other hand, is a sly venture into other spaces, perhaps an adventure into sly spaces, a theory given with full knowledge that it might be wrong, proposed for "scientific reasons." A theory that is highly personal, yet easily disowned.

My hypothesis was revealing. It concerned the Greek gods and the pattern with which they revealed themselves to me. I had once read a book by Hubert Dreyfus that discussed the ontological changes that the ancient Greeks believed they underwent when their god visited and possessed them; Stephen Fry had felt the same way, and so did I. My theory felt grand, academic, literary, and thin. However, my analyst never disagreed; instead, he let me run with it; he let it run its course. Articulating this personal theory, hypothesising, and positing my lack of belief in chemical imbalances or other default explanations helped me see things that I didn't know I knew, my relationship with the invisible, and my desire to be possessed.

I began using this question as a tool, a torch, guiding me to new associations, to unknown knowns. In analysis, I had started talking about my relationship with my sibling, a troubled relationship, full of anger, ignorance, and disproportionate reactions. For years, I had profoundly disliked him, almost not believing that I even had

DOI: 10.4324/9781032637723-8

a sibling. I found him so terrible that I had wondered how he had managed to make any friends. In fact, I would even ask them why they were friends with someone like him. Importantly, I had always felt justified in my hatred, and I had the answer to *why?*: I found him superficial, an exaggerator, careless, and narcissistic. He was older, terribly handsome, and popular, and had completely ignored me at school and throughout my childhood, further proof, in my head, of his deep and despicable self-involvement. However, I knew many people who were similar to him, and I didn't despise them in the same way. I didn't clench my fists when those people spoke, I didn't ignore them for months on end, and I didn't talk terribly about them to other people. I was wondering why I had such an unreasonable reaction to him when my analyst asked for my hypothesis.

> I don't know. Why would he ignore me? Was I that unnecessary? Was I that invisible?
> *Silence.*
> I guess I can't know why he'd ignore me. But I could look at what it might have done to me.
> *Done to you?*
> Yeah, it must have hurt.
> *Silence.*
> It must have hurt because I must have really wanted his love.
> *Hmm.*
> I would have been so happy, so powerful, so visible if I had his love. I've actually never imagined that I might have wanted his attention, but it seems obvious – how could I not? He's my brother.
> *Let's stop there for today.*

In this short exchange with my analyst, I had completed a sentence – *It must have hurt* with a hypothesis – *because I must have really wanted his love*. I didn't know if it was true; I didn't know or remember feeling or wanting love from my brother as a child; I don't remember deciding to hate him either. However, by venturing this hypothesis, which didn't feel too improbable, I entered into a new story, a richer, more compassionate story in which I actually loved him, and therefore wanted his love. I felt certain chains of anger drop from my wrists, and I felt a desire to talk to him and to make him my brother again.

However, I wondered why my analyst had stopped the session at that exact moment. I had said something real, fallen into a moment of fullness, when he said *Let's stop there today*. I think this was his intervention. I walked out with a rush of new feeling that was all my own, that needed to be my own. I was in possession of feelings for my sibling –feelings that didn't belong in the clinic with my analyst. They belonged with me, and perhaps with my brother.

Analysis hadn't given me any answers. My analyst hadn't offered an interpretation. Instead, in that space, within that relationship, my own theories about my life and my history were allowed to run, to be right or wrong, to achieve or lose meaning, and to be reconstituted. I wouldn't say that I had stopped thinking about Greek gods or that my relationship with my brother is fully healed. However, they possess less power over me. I have ventured into a new space where I have a little more freedom, potentially an opportunity, and perhaps some love.

A Thread of Interpretation

I started my analysis almost four years ago and like many others who choose to cross the threshold of an analyst's office, a certain amount of suffering accompanied and motivated my visit. Since my early teen years, I felt somewhat disillusioned from life, and I rarely encountered anything that would excite me or give me a lasting sense of purpose. Love partners and relationships were proving themselves to be less worthy than my initial estimations, and the prestigious diploma I had acquired from my university left me totally unmoved and without any wish to pursue a job in this discipline. In an attempt to change this situation, I moved to London to start a Masters, while hoping that this would bring something different to my life. Indeed, after some time, I met a woman who though our relationship brought a sense of meaning and joy back into my life, though after a few years and to my dismay she ended the relationship. At that point I was even more disheartened than before, feeling that despite my efforts, there was no one I could trust to have a meaningful relationship and life could only bring disappointment.

With such thoughts weighing me down, I had walked into my analysis and expected from this person we call the psychoanalyst to tell me the reason why I am feeling like this and change my perspective. So after communicating to him the issues I was facing, I sat silent and was waiting for his solution. Instead of giving me any kind of solution, he said that he knows barely anything about me and encouraged me to speak about my history. I started speaking about my past and my childhood, and during these first months of being in analysis, I remember one of his earliest interventions. I was recalling a childhood memory, and without noticing I said 'Back then, when I was still alive, I…' and continued my sentence, but he interrupted me drawing my attention to what I had just said. When I became aware of the slip of the tongue, I was surprised by the paradox I had brought to the surface. On the one hand, how is it possible that I am sitting here and talking about something if I am already dead? and, on the other hand, it seemed funny to me as I, unknowingly yet perhaps accurately, had depicted my disenchantment with life as being already dead.

This contradiction stuck with me, yet for the time being I did not return to it. I kept narrating all the different examples and experiences I had, which would serve as evidence for my world view and the hopeless state of life. More contradictions

DOI: 10.4324/9781032637723-9

emerged within this narrative, some picked up by my analyst and some by myself as I was speaking. After more than a year had passed, my analyst commented that the point is not to find proof that validates my perspective on life but to see why I adopted this perspective in the first place, whereas another person could have formulated a different response than mine. This comment startled me: how would it be possible for someone to have a different response? Nevertheless, I know, and knew back then as well, that people may be exposed to the same experiences but will react and respond in different ways. Perhaps what I was searching for, the reason that would explain and justify my current situation, was never there to begin with. Hence, there must have always been a decision made on my part. I remembered the slip I mentioned earlier and how it already revealed a choice, the choice to live as dead. A choice I had taken which crystallised life under a specific facet and was now illuminating my path in life. Despite knowing and admitting that life is not unidimensional, I had adopted a point of view that was filtering life in a very unilateral way. The contradictions that emerged in analysis helped me to crack this prism I had constructed and show the possibility of change.

I was recently contemplating the change I have experienced so far owing to my personal analysis, and the words that came to my mind were that I am learning how to live life all over again. Through psychoanalysis I now have a language with which to speak about certain things that previously was not there. In this way of speaking well, I am able to provide a safe harbour from my anxiety and venture outside the port at times. The experience of contradicting myself in analysis during my attempts to defend my fantasy has made me more willing to accept the contradictions that are inherent in life itself. Lastly, the need to adopt an all-encompassing perspective with which I can confront the vicissitudes of life is mitigated, because through the contradictions I present in analysis, I come to realise in practice that 'there is no truth that, passing through awareness, does not lie'.

Analysis, Moments of Concluding

An analysis is really a series of moments, as Lacan (1945) described in his essay on logical time. He specified three moments – the instant of seeing, the time of understanding, and the moment to conclude – which divide up the progress of an analysis into three distinctive phases. But in describing these phases as moments, Lacan reminds us that a shift of phase in an analysis is often one of unadulterated momentariness and instantaneity of timing. These co-constructed moments between analysand and analyst, when something new emerges and there's a real shift in perspective, are typically unplanned and come as bolts out of the blue which can stun or overwhelm before settling into new avenues of articulation. Or these moments can emerge more slowly and discretely when, under the sway of an interpretation or new material (from a memory, signifier, association, parapraxis, or affective response), elements that no longer fit or simply no longer work are revealed. This is a dialectical process in which what is known comes to be amended and rescripted by new material and, as an ongoing rolling process punctuated by various "conclusions" with stops and breaks, can be temporary or more permanent. This is all very general. I will now get more specific.

I've been through two analyses, each with a different analyst and the concluding moment in each has been very different. I would say each analysis roughly corresponded with interrogating my relationship with my mother and with my father in that order. My first analysis, a training analysis, was with a woman whom I chose on the basis of her name which sounded foreign and seemed to fit with my own sense and experience of being different. Importantly, she never "othered" me as I expected, even when I tried on occasion to force it by saying scandalous things and trying to provoke a reaction from her. I got nothing in return and was instead escorted into the terrain of my own family mythologies and neuroses which my own perceived sense of "difference," including a long time spent living abroad in foreign lands, had not in fact distanced me from. Confrontations with the oddities of my family and my profoundly difficult lifelong relationship with my mother who hated my "difference" were possible with this analyst who would not be baited into being consigned the role of my hating mother, all done unconsciously of course. This "conclusion" was a time of understanding.

DOI: 10.4324/9781032637723-10

The analysis settled into supporting my own developing practice and identity as a psychoanalytic practitioner which I was initially very tentative and unsure about. I decided in some ways to postpone any decision about that by embarking on a further course of academic study, during which I continued with my little erstwhile practice. The "outsider" status of psychoanalysis and that of "psychoanalyst" grew on me and came to satisfy a jouissance attached to the signification of being different and outside the mainstream. I became more active in the local psychoanalytic group, increasingly so as the years went on, even becoming somewhat prominent in its activities. I quit my undesirable day job and with it my main source of income, and slowly but surely psychoanalysis became my main preoccupation. With that my practice began to grow and increasingly became important. My father's occupation was one that included a "practice," and I began to recognise a certain overlap with his desire. Some years after this analysis finished, when pondering one day the length of time it took me to complete my further studies, it hit me that I'd taken exactly the same length of time as my father took to complete his meandering studies, studies that eventually allowed him to "practice." It took a long time, he said, due to being seriously involved in sport, succeeding to international level once, just as I had, on one occasion.

This re-scripting of my meandering journey through my studies to a practice functioned as a hinge to subsequent conclusions. In my second analysis, several conclusions came to light. I came to reckon with an identification with my grandmother whose name I carry quietly as a second name and who was a wandering independent soul who sent her children away to school from a young age and separated from my grandfather when this was very rarely done. She lived happily and successfully outside of the mainstream and was a kind of roving spirit.

My second analysis, undertaken seven years after the conclusion of my first analysis and subsequent to the death of a sibling and my beloved father, allowed me to conclude that my mother's desire was not a desire for marriage and children but a thwarted desire for a profession she gave up when she married my father and had three children at a very young age. I've never had a desire for children. It transpired that both of my parents' blood types were "incompatible," and this meant that my mother endured three difficult pregnancies and births. In addition, my father contracted German measles in early adolescence and had been told he'd never have children. I was therefore not only a surprise for both of my parents but one that created great trouble for my mother.

As if unsure about whether I was a blessing or a curse, my father named me after both a character in a well-known film and the actor that played her. He said he wasn't quite sure which it was, and the name of the actor and character's role are almost identical. In the famous film role, the character is both good and bad, although good ultimately triumphs. To this day, hardly a month goes by when my name is not mis-said as the actor's name, underscoring another "concluding." I was, to some extent, an imaginary character, not quite real, to my father, and he struggled to know me. Adding to this, I look nothing like him or my mother, not one bit, although I do bear some small resemblance to certain members of the family on her side.

My second analyst, who was very experienced and had in fact taught on my clinical training programme, was very important to me as he was the first to encourage me to write and publish, to what I call "produce." He was quite reluctant to do that himself, much like my own father, who'd never had the confidence to bring his practice, for which he was revered, to the academy and teach it in spite of being invited to do so but who, like this analyst, was an excellent practitioner. While I never managed to supersede my father and go beyond once representing my country in sport, these days I spend a lot of time teaching in addition to practicing.

Love as an Effect of Truth

How does change happen in analysis? I've had two experiences of Lacanian analysis: the first very classical, with ultra short sessions and interpretations that often took the form of verbal ambiguities, and the second quite different, with much longer sessions and interventions that either posed questions or suggested meanings to make sense of the material. Both experiences had their effects, even if these effects did not always go in the same direction.

Having seen analysis in the movies and read case histories, when I started I was expecting moments of sudden illumination, moments when some secret is revealed and the pieces of the jigsaw fit into place. There were certainly moments like this, yet usually they happened outside the actual sessions: reading a psychoanalytic text I'd make a connection or talking to a friend I'd realise something. Arguably, the mobilisation of the unconscious within the analytic work was what allowed such links to be made outside it.

For example, I spent an excessive amount of money pursuing a particular sporting activity, which I often mentioned during sessions, yet it was never explored or interpreted, although it was clear, it constituted some sort of acting out. Only much later on, I suddenly saw that the expression used to refer to the activity was a very obvious anagram of the name of one of my parents.

This was a moment of illumination, and I was surprised and remember laughing out loud at the connection. Did it change my relation to the activity at the time? Not in any obvious sense, and looking back, these translation moments when a truth becomes evident did not really have lasting results or change much. One thing I did notice was that when they occasionally happened within sessions, they would generate a momentary feeling of love or gratitude towards the analyst: love as an effect of truth.

The changes that did result from that first experience of analysis were probably on the side of identifications. I became better at what I did and more confident, largely through a kind of mimicry of the analyst. I did my best to please, to be the good analysand, and the analyst's efforts to undermine this were not entirely successful, as they themselves mimicked – perhaps deliberately – the educational efforts of my own upbringing. Short sessions seemed to reinforce this process

DOI: 10.4324/9781032637723-11

of identification rather than work against it. So I'd say that the direction of that first analysis was towards identification, even if this undoubtedly had therapeutic effects. I could inhabit the identifications more easily, although the basic underlying problems were, I think, unresolved.

My second experience was very different. To start with, the analyst asked me questions about my life and my family history. I realised that in the first analysis, despite the fact it had lasted several years, there had not been a single question about family history or childhood, as if what came out of free association was the only thing to go on. But now there was much more of a work of construction, facilitated by the analyst's questions and comments. Also, I did not feel that I had to prove anything, to be a good analysand, but was trying to tackle problems that were making daily life a struggle.

I found that this more 'biographical' work was fruitful in many ways. It not only allowed a new perspective on my own life historically, but it generated dreams and memories through this process that brought out key dynamics from infancy and childhood that were central to the problems I was having as an adult. I also felt that my analyst was actually interested in the work, and not just playing the part of a Lacanian and doing what Lacanians are supposed to do. Their interventions were put forward in a tentative way, like conjectures, rather than as statements that I had to agree with or accept, as had been the case at times in the earlier analysis.

Was there some particular intervention that changed everything? I don't think so – it was more the slow process of piecing things together and then realising where they couldn't be, the points where questions could not be answered or certain facts would forever remain out of reach. I would say that the real factors causing change here were the analyst's interest, as shown, for example, through the process of posing questions and offering occasional interpretations, which made a certain kind of work possible.

The end of both analyses was marked by the production of dreams. In the first, two verbal dreams, each consisting of just a single enigmatic expression, semantically rich despite the minimalism. One evoked an action, the other the consequence of an action, yet the meaning, what the action had been, was left opaque. They were both quite funny, like punchlines of jokes, results of condensations. With the second analysis, the dreams at the end were visual and not immediately verbal: empty desolate landscapes, indexing both a psychical situation and a change in phantasies about the body that had been part of the work in the previous months.

After this second analysis, I found the pull of identifications less powerful. I was less concerned with what others thought about me, and less bothered about cultivating an image. I was more interested, in a sense, in my own interests, some of which of course had their antecedents in childhood while some were newer and more recent. And the old acting out activity? I would still do it every so often, though now in the company of friends, and no longer compulsively. And the feelings it generated were less contradictory.

So analysis had effects, substantial and enduring ones. I don't see it as a process with some particular predetermined result, and am open to engaging again in the future if the need arises. What life brings can never be predicted, and as Freud said, external events can be the occasion to return to analysis as and when. We can never really know how we will cope with loss and change, and this remains a challenge for each of us.

We Have a Date!

During the tobacco harvesting season, he sometimes worked the night shift to oversee the tobacco curing in the barn. I slept in the house next door.

One night, I woke up to find him sitting on the side of my bed, touching my nipple and clitoris. I didn't move; I pretended to be asleep. He left, and then I fell asleep. I don't remember anything about the day after.

My first recollection of this scene was when I put it into words for the first time; four years later, when I was 16 years old, I told a friend what had happened.

Although I've always wondered why I pretended to be asleep, I never really questioned it until almost two years into my analysis, when I fell ill with breast cancer. I connected the illness to my inability to articulate the distress I'd carried with me all these years.

I hadn't seen him for 12 years, during which time we had only sporadic contact via text. When I told him I was ill, he replied, 'I'm sorry about what happened. Take care, have faith, and everything will work out! If someone in the family had the problem, we could say it was hereditary, but that's not the case.'

Enraged, I replied, 'No, this is not hereditary – this is because I never had the courage to speak up about what you did to me. I remember that night when you crossed a line no one should ever cross. The fact that I never spoke up caused this to happen to me. Why did you abuse me when I was sleeping?'

In response, he said I was crazy and that he hadn't done what I was accusing him of; it was all in my head. He asked me to prove it. That was the last time we spoke to each other.

Consequently, I questioned the entire reality I'd been living up until that moment. I had no evidence; the only thing I had was my distorted memory, four years of selective amnesia, and the effects on my body.

Around this time, I became more familiar with psychoanalytic literature and did a lot of research on Freud's theory of seduction – and his abandonment of the theory saying he'd made a mistake; that his patients' memories of sexual abuse were, in fact, phantasies of being seduced in childhood.

My being became consumed by the question: *Am I making up a story about being sexually abused, creating a whole reality around a memory that isn't even true?*

DOI: 10.4324/9781032637723-12

In analysis, I was able to remember and talk through the relationship I had with him, where words were missing, and explore the prevailing theme of obedience.

I heard my analyst say, 'He replied quickly with such certainty,' which helped me elaborate on other questions and construct something solid, rather than believing I'd invented false memories. I'd told him he'd sexually abused me, and he'd denied it only once. Faced with such an accusation, it's assumed that one would want to have more details so they could defend themselves.

My analyst's interpretations were directed at moments of repetition – falling in love with an older or unattainable man, and other scenes of seduction that I'd encountered throughout my life.

Two crucial moments in analysis.

The first was a dream.

It was night, and I was walking, alone, along the main street of my hometown towards the primary school I used to go to. I passed the bakery where I used to buy bread on the way to school. On the way back to the main square, I went to the toilet in the old hotel. I put my iPhone by the window before using the toilet, then left and kept walking. I found myself at a bus stop 60 kilometres away and realised I didn't have my iPhone with me. I became desperate, wondering how I could have lost it.

By sunrise, I'd remembered where I'd left it, and I wanted to go back to get it. There was no bus in those early hours, so I decided to walk back. I was in a panic, thinking about what I would do without my iPhone – all the memories it held, my contacts, emails, notes, and photos.

After some time walking, however, I realised that my iPhone had been in my hand the whole time. In one hand, I held the iPhone, and in the other, the house keys to my current house.

My analyst said something like 'The lost memory' – I'm not sure exactly, but whatever I heard made sense to me. I was able to connect my not-lost iPhone to the memory I was putting in doubt. These days, our smartphones are also places where memories are kept, and I thought I'd lost mine against the outside knowledge from (the father of) psychoanalysis.

The second was a slip of the tongue.

In one session, while talking about the surgeries I'd undergone, I said that the first surgery was in August, and the second in January – but I meant to say that the second was in September, not in January. After a brief silence, I heard from my analyst, 'We have a date.'

'It was indeed January, during the tobacco curing season,' I said. I only realised I'd covered my body with my jacket during the session when my analyst pointed it out. I got up from the couch and said I'd had enough for the day.

One does not surpass, but can instead do something with it, including psychoanalysis – *a père version*, which means 'a version of the father' in French. A father who makes mistakes, who is a fool. The names of the father (*les noms du père*). According to Lacan's French homophone (*les non-dupes errent*), this can be seen as foolishness or what might seem nonsensical, similar to the unforgettable experiences we encounter in life.

However, they can also be treated and possibly cured, much like cancer.

Bibliography

Freud, S. (1932). 'New Introductory Lectures on Psychoanalysis and Other Works'. The Standard Edition of the Complete Psychological Works of Sigmund Freud, Volume XXII (1932–1936): New Introductory Lectures on Psychoanalysis, Femininity, p. 120.
Lacan, J. (1973). Seminar XXI Les Non-Dupes Errent (1973–1974). Gallagher's Translation.

The Place of the Object

I was about six months into my analysis. Everything was going very well. Even though I had two young infants when I began my formation as an analyst, I considered that I had plenty of time to carry out the academic workload of the training (in the first instance, a two-year clinical Master's degree at the University hospital); the clinical practice requirement of the degree (at least two patients in the first year, which in my own practice actually climbed to ten in six months); the twice weekly analysis; and the weekly supervision. All of these various exigencies had me running from one end to the other of Dublin city and its suburbs (mostly on public transport), arranging childminders, and bargaining with my lovely husband and equally lovely mother, for time, baby minding, dinner cooking, etc. Getting from my house to analysis entailed a one-and-a-half-hour bus journey and then a commuter train for a further half hour, and back again. On top of this, I had three separate part-time teaching contracts. No problem! I was, always had been, ready for anything and top of my class. No matter what! I was the model student, my essays were flawless, and my thirst for knowledge unquenchable. My fellow students teased me having discovered how nerdy I was and at the same time genuinely looked on in awe as I juggled babies, assignments, and work. I soon developed a kind of status of class 'expert'; if the course lecturers threw out a seemingly impossible question to the group, the group would turn to me expectantly: she must know? I was somehow simultaneously the eponymous Rita from 'Educating Rita' and Elle Woods from 'Legally Blonde'.

At the same time, my youngest child – still a baby really – had been developing a symptom: a nightly cough that kept us all awake. Many nights consisted of me sleeping half sitting up with the baby propped up against my chest to ease his breathing. Every three weeks, I was running to the general physician for yet another antibiotic which I hated to administer, having breastfed him for the first 18 months of his life to try to ensure a robust immune system. Why then was he so unwell? Some six months into my analysis, my husband and I had finally got an appointment with a paediatric asthma specialist who diagnosed our baby with infantile asthma.

Then I had a dream.

I brought my baby to the asthma specialist, and while waiting to be called for the appointment, my mobile phone rang and it was my GP calling. She asked me,

DOI: 10.4324/9781032637723-13

'Did they tell you what it is?' I replied, 'No, not yet'. She continued, 'They have been in touch with me and guess what?' 'What?' I asked. 'It's not asthma, its 'incopedia'.

I brought the dream to my analyst who hmm-hemmed a good deal over this funny signifying neologism which I immediately broke up into three: *In – co – pedia*. 'In' simply referred to 'in'; 'co' was me, my very name condensed into its initials and part of the nickname my eldest brother occasionally used for me, *Coco*; and 'pedia' was a reference both to education or knowledge as in encyclopedia but also to the child as in pedia-trics. It was clear I expected to find the knowledge about my baby's condition in myself, considering my desire and jouissance at work in the acquisition of knowledge and the identity I had constructed as the one who knows so much/it all. But there was more, for also contained within this neologism was the word 'cope', and it was precisely around coping with my lack of knowledge of my child's condition and my essential lack that thus far had gone unexamined and therefore unanalysed.

The dream caused a questioning around lack, my place as an object of knowledge, and the jouissance in knowing, which – as with most jouissance – was never satisfied, often ending in a suffering.

In the last session of my analysis, many years later, my meanderings led me to a strange 'not-knowing', a little piece of nonsense, some silly reflection on how I just realised that I never knew the actual, precise address (place?) of the analyst, after all this time. Some laughter. A lot of surprise. The last three words I uttered there: 'I don't know'.

Fathers and Daughters

One transference-altering moment in my analysis involves an interpretation which I suspect wasn't, in fact, an interpretation. What's more, it was this suspicion, rather than the 'interpretation' as such, that produced an effect.

I entered one day to find my analyst hunched over, holding his left side, limping painfully to and from each door he ushered me into. Tellingly, my first thought was that this was an intervention – he must be performing a kind of lack. I was sure that his injury had a slightly fictitious air, not dissimilar to the physical contortion of a beggar who bends and shakes in order to appear gravely wounded. Immediately after this thought came another: how absurd that upon seeing my analyst injured, I mutate what is right in front of me into some elaborate interpretation under his control, so sure am I that he could never be afflicted with such fragility. Then a third thought: if he is indeed injured, there is now the compulsion to save him from the shame which could arise out of my pity at his predicament. The three thoughts combined to produce my response: I completely ignored that anything altogether different was happening. I dutifully went straight to the couch, as I had done for so many years, lay down, free associated, then left. As the door closed behind me, I began to laugh.

My own history appeared as if in a dreamscape before my eyes. I had felt the same compulsion to my father and brother, both of whose presences I had felt, until this moment, as persecutory figures who critiqued and belittled me. It was clear now how diligently I had been working to keep them in that position, namely as figures who had something I did not. My analyst must have been aiming at this, I mutter to myself, unwittingly reinstating him as an all-knowing, infallible presence. But then the image of his disfigurement would flash up, and the memory of my flaccid reaction, my quiet horror, at this uncanny figure. Why should this be something I strive not to see?

It was as though just at the moment that I felt the transference begin to disassemble – a natural outcome to the sudden revelation of the humanity of the analyst – I gave myself to the task of holding the illusion together. The effect, more through the glittering irony of this string of responses than through a straightforward receipt of a message, was the realization of my part in the transference fantasy, which in turn slowly loosened it. But – crucially – in my own hesitant, and

DOI: 10.4324/9781032637723-14

occasionally regressive, time. Still today, the whole affair has gone unspoken, and I cringe at the prospect of offering my sympathy, or asking what had happened, or worse, assisting him as he limped to and fro. My discomfort at this prospect evidently reveals a continued investment in keeping him slightly elevated. I always think now of the stories children tell one another of how big, how accomplished, their daddies are. The passionate protection of a structure in which you are kept subordinate is a strange component of identification, particularly between fathers and daughters – one which, even if it reveals itself, can be so tempting to preserve.

Lateness

Vignette 1

During my psychoanalytic sessions, I found myself exploring stories that seemed to have no connection to my initial symptoms. It was during one of these sessions that my legendary tardiness made an appearance. Picture this: I arrived, as usual, fashionably late, only to discover my psychoanalyst standing at the door, bags packed and ready for a well-deserved holiday. Perhaps my tears and desperation compelled my therapist to abandon their getaway and attend, once again, to my emotional turmoil.

My lateness was never without a reason or, shall I say, unmotivated. There were instances where I got utterly, truly lost on my way, transforming a simple commute into a grand drama. It seemed and it felt as if life conspired to test my punctuality at every turn. Nevertheless, my psychoanalyst, who presented as a patient soul and listened to my reasons, never sanctioned my lateness, offering me instead the possibility to catch my breath in a cafe close by before coming back to the practice and dive into the core of my session.

And so, one day, I embarked on a storytelling journey, exploring the intricate web of my lineage, my family's complex dynamics, and my dear mother's complicated pregnancies. It was as if I had opened a treasure trove of Gordian narratives, each shedding light on the tapestry of my existence.

But let me not stray too far into the intricacies of my mother's pregnancies. Instead, let us remember that within these stories lay the secrets, the quirks, singularities, twists, and the unconscious peculiarities that have shaped my inclination for lateness. Through the lens of psychoanalysis, I discovered that even seemingly unrelated anecdotes can hold profound meaning and offer valuable insights into our inner selves.

So, as I continued on this therapeutic journey, I used to arrive consistently late at my appointments. One day, during a session, I began discussing my family structure and stumbled upon the topic of my mother's pregnancies. It turned out that when I was six and seven years old, my mother had been pregnant twice, but she intentionally miscarried. As I explored this topic with my psychoanalyst, it became apparent that I had been caught up in these family dramas and these difficult

DOI: 10.4324/9781032637723-15

circumstances. As a child, I desperately wanted my mother to keep the babies, which led to feelings of guilt. My analyst interpreted the situation, explaining that it wasn't solely about my mother's pregnancies and miscarriages but rather about the fact that I had actively participated in these discussions. One session concluded with my comment about feeling guilty for coming into existence too early. Since then, I have no longer been late for my appointments.

Vignette 2

After two years of intense psychoanalysis, during which I may have shattered the sound barrier – on the edge of shouting at each session, I spent my time portraying a member of my family as the epitome of evil – malicious, two-faced, a liar, unloving and uncaring, unwise and inconsiderate, selfish and excluding, egocentric and torturing, corrupted and persecutory, harmful and full of hate – a prodigious inventory of baseness and corruption.

And then, one fateful day, the élan in the consulting room radically shifted. It was as if the very fabric of my analysis had been rewoven; the whole circuit of anxiety rewired. In the following sessions, a word appeared after the "sudden" fading of the object of my complaint: "Subjectivation". I had yet to learn whether this word even existed in a dictionary. And truth be told, I am still clueless about my actual understanding of it.

I don't remember if there had been a crucial moment. Or a striking intervention by my psychoanalyst, which helped me shift my position from being victimised to untangling the threads of my enjoyment. What I do remember are those interventions during which the psychoanalyst cut the session, precisely at a moment of refusal of unlimited enjoyment. I vividly recall the lack I experienced in relation to language. With hindsight, it was a desperate yearning to connect with something that seemed absent. Back then, it was possibly a sense of spirituality or a deeper understanding of my connection with language itself. But I also separated myself from what ultimately encapsulated my unique expression most profoundly – poetry. I also remember that particular session where the word "subjectivation" came about – something I needed desperately.

The Fruit, the Vagina and the Pyjamas

I once had a dream where my face had spontaneously grown two fig-shaped fruits which were oddly velvety and hanging off it. This made me feel shocked, ashamed and really uncomfortable. Imagine going round with a slightly hairy huge double-thing hanging off your face! I wanted it taken off as soon as possible! These strong feelings prevailed sometime after the dream had happened. My immediate interpretation during my psychoanalytic session was related to ambivalence towards my loved ones. After the end of the session, when we were saying our usual goodbyes, my analyst then added a surprising: 'Have a nice day!' said with an almost imperceptible mocking tone. This simple yet slightly off addition made me wonder why it was there then. When I tried to think about it, I found myself firstly, a bit angry and then laughing. Doesn't Freud say that in dreams, anything on the face is genitalia? I think this: 'Have a nice day!' was a brilliant interpretation mainly for its ambiguity. The analyst did not say: 'You wish for male genitalia, so you gave it to yourself in the dream. Now go have a nice time with it!' Spelling it all out for me would have only promoted resistance against this meaning. Instead, it was its vagueness which welcomed my own deduction. I did feel a bit of anger which is a form of resistance (though anger is not always resistance in analysis). However, this was overcome swiftly as the interpretation had been my own. I think that by bringing the 'Have a nice day!' unexpectedly and accompanied by humour invited an otherwise impossible unveiling. What followed in the work was a revelation of unconscious sexual ambiguities and contradictions as well as their powerful impact on the different roles (both assumed and inhibited) in my life.

So, ambiguity in interpretations can be productive in the work. But, is there any case when the opposite is to be chosen in the technique instead? When I was young and living in a different country to England, my psychoanalyst was also my teacher both at university and in a Lacanian reading group. This meant we would see each other very often (maybe every day including part of the weekend!) so I knew him well. He was someone I could fully trust. Back then, I now know, I was overwhelmed by fear and guilt around sexuality and yet, and I was not sure what the problem really was. Was it that there was something truly missing or was I not being appreciative enough of what I did have in my life? Should I wait for things to happen naturally for me or should I go and get them? I wanted to go out

DOI: 10.4324/9781032637723-16

and feel confident, I wanted to be desirable, to be considered attractive, perhaps to be in a relationship too, etc.... Though I cannot remember the particulars of this session I want to talk about, I do remember my analyst's exact interpretation: 'You want to be penetrated', he clearly stated. Certainly daring in its delivery, it had a profoundly liberating effect on me. I believe that the paternal place that my analyst occupied for me in the work – as well as, and perhaps crucially, the mutual trust between us – gave me permission to see myself as a sexed woman. Most importantly, the sexual desire to be enjoyed as a woman – which had been previously blocked by religious and social preconceptions, fears, prohibitions and years of denial of the vagina in my upbringing – could finally start blossoming. The fact that this was said unambiguously seemed to have done the trick for me. After this analysis, I was able to leave the parental home for the first time and to further my knowledge abroad.

Let us dive into the fascinating use of theatre in analysis. Fast-forwarding some years ahead, during preliminary sessions with a male analyst, and after leaving a long analysis with a female analyst, I produced a dream. 'I arrive at his consulting room, find the door ajar and inside there is only a dim light on. I nervously come in and sit in the waiting room. It all feels mysterious and is so quiet, and it is unsettling. I wait, and wait, and wait some more; but no one is coming. I then realise I have been forgotten in my analyst's waiting room as night suddenly falls and darkness inundates the place. My anxiety grows now, less from having been forgotten, but for being where I should not presently be as it is at a very inappropriate time. It is so late! What if I bump into him in his pyjamas on my way out?' When the analyst asks what I make of the dream I – on the basis of the dream being a wish – shyly reply with a question: 'Do I want to see you in your PJs?'. Session ends and he then asks to see me the following day: 'Come late, very late'. No time is set until I get a text the following day late in the evening: 'Come at 8pm'. I arrive to find very much a restaging of my dream. The door is ajar, lights are off, it is all so quiet and certainly feels mysterious! He then makes me wait, and wait, and wait some more; with no movement or sound around. When he finally appears, he invites me into the consulting room but instead of letting me pass ahead as would be usual, he suddenly cuts my way by going before me. I therefore can now see his back and most shockingly, his pyjama-like pants tucked awkwardly, even ridiculously – all the way up on top of his shirt. This bold theatrical arrangement based on my own dream interpretation was in that moment an invitation to start with the analysis of my desire. It was almost as if it were saying: 'Okay, it is alright, here's the PJs. Now, what is it that you really want?' I believe that this audacious psychoanalytic act was also, and perhaps crucially, declaring the analyst's unashamed involvement in what was the commencement of a work of collaboration. Here again the dynamic of trust between us is generous and very much essential. A psychical separation from my father was one of the consequences of this labour together, as well as the eruption of a desire to have children with my partner. Around a year after this striking adventure, I was entering another by becoming a mother for the first time.

In fact, this psychoanalytic act has been used throughout the work as an invaluable tool: like a motif illuminating central themes in music through its repetition. In moments of depression, it has sometimes had the force of lifting me up even if slightly. If guilt surrounding sexual matters re-emerges, it sometimes has had the power of appeasing it. If I feel I am losing confidence in myself, it has sometimes acted as a hook to keep me going. As the analysis progresses, it evolves with it yet maintaining its essence. Could we see this aspect of the work as privileged, singled-out through its theatrical quality, as the holder of the foundations in the relationship of collaboration that is required in our analytic work?

Hidden in Plain Sight

A year after I started analysis, I was on my way to the session with the idea of interrupting the work. A few weeks prior, I had tentatively asked: "How does one end therapy?". My analyst replied that every ending is unique and up for discussion. During the short walk to the practice, I revisited my rationale. I was in a much better place than I used to be in, most of my symptomatic formations had receded, and I was moderately adjusted to life. At the same time, I felt that the work was going nowhere. Sessions had become repetitive and devoid of insight, and I found it difficult to bring fresh material. This was in marked opposition to what, since the very beginning, made me voraciously engage with the process – namely the surprise effect that my own speech had upon me (and crucially, I can now add, that it seemed to have on my analyst, whom I could not bear to bore). At the same time, I sensed that something significant remained unaddressed. Perhaps this would only be a pause, and the work could resume in the future. Finally, as we were approaching a scheduled break, it seemed like a "natural" time to end.

I sat down in front of the analyst and began laying out my ideas. After a moment of silence, the analyst said: "Interrupting the work is certainly a possibility, but you could also move to the couch". She turned her head to the left. I followed her gaze, landing on the Le Corbusier chaise longue. I was surprised to find it there. Even though it had always been right in front of me, facing the window and away from the analyst's gaze, I had never fully acknowledged its presence. It had always just been a piece of furniture, an ornament, perhaps a homage to psychoanalytic history. An image rather than a place. I had formed the conviction that the couch was only used by old-fashioned Freudians, working on a minimum of four sessions a week in some elegant New York office. I later discovered that this idea was my own creation, but at the time I was sure I had read it somewhere, that it was common sense even. I remember quite vividly the uncanny effect that the sight of the couch produced. I felt disoriented. I did not confess that I did not "believe" in the couch as it would have meant to acknowledge that I did not (want to) believe in the unconscious. Instead, I mumbled: "The couch… Right… And what would working on the couch entail?" "Well, it may help with free association, shifting the focus away from practical concerns". After a few moments of silence, I heard

DOI: 10.4324/9781032637723-17

myself speaking with renewed excitement: "Sounds great, after the break I'll move to the couch".

During the break, I had the following dream: I am at my hometown's football stadium. An army of young soldiers – about my age, clean shaved – are training on the pitch. They move in perfect unison under the orders of an older captain. I see a door, half-open, leading to a swimming pool I used to go to as a child. As I walk down the stairs, I realise that I have arrived somewhere else – a slum, mostly inhabited by foreigners who fled war and hardship – hidden under the stadium. There are families and children living in barracks made of cardboard. I wonder: "How come no one has discovered it until now? It was so easy for me to reach". Speaking to a woman, I gather that they have been hidden there by corrupt government officials. I tell her that what they are experiencing is unfair, and they deserve better living conditions. She replies that life is horrible down there, but if the news were to spread, there could be devastating repercussions. I suddenly realise that I have a choice to make. The following thought is formed: "Only a serious investigative journalist could do justice to the situation. Could I ever become one? Do I have enough integrity to face this truth?". I wake up in a state of intense anxiety.

This dream became an important reference point in my analysis for years to come. I will not unpack the numerous associative threads woven into the dream's text. Just one observation: the journey from the well-organised stadium (the conscious mind) to an unknown locus where a foreign language is spoken (the unconscious) is as instructive as it is potentially deceptive. Following Freud's insights, I came to realise how important it is not to be overly seduced by the dream's narrative pathos, privileging single details, structural relations, and formal impasses instead (and why not, alternative plotlines: for instance, what if we reverse a dream's temporality, reading it from end to beginning?). Besides the interpretative work it elicited over time, what gave this dream a special status in my analysis is that it marked an attempt to inscribe a shift of positioning. I would not however reduce the shift to a movement from A to B, from chair to couch, from therapy to analysis, from stadium to slum. That would miss an important point, namely that the dream primarily concerns the articulation of a question. How to deal with that which is in plain sight yet invisible, within reach yet inaccessible, intimate yet ob-scene? The couch, the slum, the unconscious: in the session as well as the dream, the Other Scene does not manifest as a far-removed depth, but as a poorly disguised object, an (un)familiar place, an unknown knowledge. A form of questioning implicating the subject may then emerge: how could I have ignored something so evidently placed under my nose? What mode of satisfaction does this entail? Might this "passion for ignorance" constitute the other side of a desire to know? And if so, can I take responsibility for their entanglement?

A final reflection to point out how the analyst's intervention exemplifies an essential dimension of analytic interpretation. The aim is less to attribute the correct meaning to an enigmatic formation than to send the analysand their own message back in an inverted form, echoing what in the subject speaks beyond what is intended. This can be done by pointing to something hidden in plain sight, playing with equivocation, or shifting punctuation. Timing is also crucial. Interpreting at the "right" time: when it is least expected, and yet an opening is in sight, "ending" may be heard as "beginning". You say that you want to interrupt the work, but might your desire be to raise the stakes? Might your intention to end be the expression of a desire to really begin?

Reunion

It's surprising how little of what's been said in my analysis I can remember now. Geographical points and their subjective resonance sound crucial in my process, really. The relation between spaces and tongues seemed to be more relevant in time than the act of speaking "alone". I chose my analyst according to two dimensions: the location of his consulting room and the fact that he was French-speaking. These two conditions sufficed for transference to be established. Actually, for a long time psychoanalysis felt like talking alone somewhere in the presence of somebody daunting, who I now see as a kind of colleague, despite the fact that he will always remain "my analyst" somehow.

Travelling from the other side of the world, from the other side of the Channel, and from the other side of London (where I lived for ten years) to have half-an-hour sessions once, twice then three times a week in "zone 1" was like a fort-da game following my mum's footsteps, i.e. the young woman my mother would have been before meeting my dad in Paris and later becoming "somebody else". I have long been inhabited by representations of my parents' stories preceding my birth.

The analytic consulting room was a few steps away from a familiar place associated with my mum and to my then boyfriend (who was hosted in the same students' house as my mother, a generation later). The visibly present synagogue on the way to the analyst's place from the tube station also made a difference. It was precisely what my dad had not transmitted, which in fact hadn't really been transmitted to him either. With a missing (name of a) father of/for my father and a fur coat made in Paris, I had to go further to map things out and stitch something up in and on my own way with this Unknown.

French as my "father tongue" was the medium through which my odd relation to myself as forever foreign was going to tie itself to the Other language that English represented: a language whose resonances don't affect the body in the ways "pater-maternal" tongues do (cf. Barbara Cassin in "Eloge de la traduction"). So, if the address would seem to matter more than the addressee to start with, it most certainly mattered that the addressee addressed me in French, whilst being fluent in English as well. To cut a very long story short – and I don't know the extent to which my analyst's interventions played a part in this – I changed symptoms as I changed modalities of relations with my parents and my tongue(s).

DOI: 10.4324/9781032637723-18

The melancholic traits I may have extracted from my mother's underlying sadness (however covered by action and other somatic symptoms) concerning the tragic loss of her own mother when she was a young child transformed into a much more lively posture that however has to bear a tendency to feel angry/hungry/ Hungary.

Indeed, the polyphony here condenses an identification with traits from my mother (we're both hypoglycaemic, but she's diabetic and I'm not), but also from my Hungarian-born Parisian paternal grandmother. A bodily revolution effected by this realisation produces this: my relation to the oral drive gets more expressive. I am subjected to an increased appetite for life, love, speaking, singing and playfully experimenting with soft sounds in the new experience of love I have been entertaining for nine years now. This marks a shift from the predominantly silent tracings I had been involved with since childhood, when reading, writing, drawing and painting seemed to also constitute multiple ways to avoid emitting the sound of my own voice, at least in public.

This inhibition of mine was perhaps directly related to my mother having long been a public speaker. As a young child, I strongly felt I was unlike her. Later on, I never wanted to be associated with her professional field. She doesn't understand much about mine – which works fine. I need her out of my way in order to get on with my life and work. Yet there is a thread I have been following, thanks to her and my Dad: a passion for art and culture. Besides, we both enjoy a sing-song. Except her voice when singing would often cover up softer voices. With this intense libido that she mediates in big ways/waves, I find myself having to keep her, or rather something of her (what for me is too much) at bay. And yet what my analyst brought back to me that I told him myself is this: the woman who happens to be my mother can also act as a kind of motor or motivating function somehow, to some extent, when I don't find it easy to get certain things moving.

I'm not sure this is so true anymore. I guess I am just allowing her to still take up that function sometimes. I suppose I was trying to justify the active part my mother still plays in my life when the cliché idea of the aim of a psychoanalysis would be to separate one from one's mother? Perhaps a sort of separation from the cause of a trop-mama happened in a paradoxical way in my case. The love encounter with a man who is exactly my mother's age and who perfectly condenses familiar and foreign dimensions has revived my appetite for life both with and besides psychoanalysis (a discourse and a professional field we share) and for sea-crossing.

I am Hung(a)ry for La Réunion. Yet being more often here than there, I hear the ways in which I treat subjective traces of *trop-ma* with a "*Lagoon*". It borders something that literally matters as a shared "*ma terre*" and "*ma mer*". The horizon drawn by the ocean to separate-relate between here, there and elsewhere is a hyphen I am keen to re-find with gusto. Eyes/I wide open.

Second Analysis

My training analyst had a very particular mode of intervening. He wouldn't say much throughout the session, but would always end on a kind of surrealist koan, somehow combining two or three things I'd mentioned. I thought he was an excellent analyst, mainly because he had the same facial hair as Freud. At the beginning of our work, I'd found him intimidating and constantly wanted to impress him, but by the end I didn't care what he thought at all – a Gold Standard Lacanian dissolution of the transference.

After a year or two, I found I was still brimming with symptoms, mostly enacted in the field of love. This time I chose a female analyst, mainly because she looked like Frida from Abba, who also looked like my Mum. From the first session, she was impressively plain spoken. I described the painful love triangle I had inserted myself into, to which she said, 'I know you already know this, but it does all sound a bit Oedipal'.

Amazingly, I didn't 'know' it at all. Or I only knew it consciously after she named it. Immediately I super-knew it. It was one of the most useful things anyone has ever said to me. These days I can tolerate a complicated love triangle with the best of them.

I suppose you might say it's a perfect example of Fenichel's idea that one analyst can sometimes prepare the way for another. He uses a joke about two brothers, the youngest of whom has to wear his older sibling's hand-me-downs. After wearing his brother's discarded suit for a week, he goes to his mother to complain that it's falling apart. His mother shouts at him, 'How come your brother made it last three years but you can't make it last three minutes?'

Either my verbose, clever clogs first analyst had perfectly prepared me to hear the simple message of my second, or my second analyst, with her kind, frank, collegiate interpretation was a far more suitable interlocutor for me.

DOI: 10.4324/9781032637723-19

Speak!

We interpret all the time. Words are always equivocal, and we will interpret what is said to us on the basis of our histories and of our experiences of those words and on the basis of the cultures in which we live, mostly without any conscious realisation that we are doing so. Our interpretations are also informed by our expectations, our hopes and wishes. What do we make of it when someone says, "I love you"? And, of course, when we describe events of the past, we do so subject to the vagaries of memory. While psychoanalysis has much to say about memory, we don't need to have studied its theories to know that what we most easily remember is the unusual, what has taken us by surprise rather than the everyday. It's difficult to recall what happened last Tuesday unless it was a day on which something out of the ordinary had occurred. What follows is my interpretation of three moments that took me by surprise from the beginning of my analysis – an analysis that took place over many years, characterised by the painfully mundane.

The first surprise: "Speak" was the first command of the analyst in response to my tears. I had come to the Lacanian clinic after a long analysis in a different tradition where I had secretly admired the stamina of my long-suffering analyst to remain mostly silent through the months I lay weeping on their couch. Clearly such avoidance and time wasting was not going to be tolerated here. This new shrink wanted to get on with it. They made no interpretation of the tears, no guesses as to what the tears might be trying to convey. To suggest, for example, that the tears were an expression of sadness or fear or anger may have elicited some words from me but would have pointed in a particular direction.

The second surprise came after a long – as I recall it now – period of complaining. My litany of complaints, the injustices, the frustrations, the failures of my parents, lovers and colleagues was greeted with an exasperated "Is there anything at all that you enjoy?" And as I described the pleasure I found in sunshine, the beach and the sea, the response came: "You've chosen a very strange place to live then". It was a statement that could be interpreted in more than one way. What I heard was an expression of exasperation that was so reminiscent of my mother. This was no case of mistaken identity, rather it was an interpretation I made that confirmed a familiar position I had taken up. It was a statement, too, that pointed to my own

DOI: 10.4324/9781032637723-20

involvement in my misery – to choose a place to live, to make a choice is active in contrast to being an object of others.

Psychoanalysis has a beginning, a middle and an end. The end of the beginning of my analysis was introduced by a surprising intervention. "Un fils perdu" was the strange interpretation from someone whose first language was clearly English and seemed to have no relation to the dream that I was recounting although it was a dream that included the image of a boy and of a French window. These words "Un fils perdu" were incomprehensible for someone who only spoke English, although my schoolgirl French recalled the difference between "fils" and "garçon". But whom was I speaking to? A complete idiot just trying to be clever? Are they learning French? Should I? Or is this some genius Lacanian who I am privileged to address? And what was meant by this silly comment? I had been told nothing that made any sense. The effects of this enigmatic statement and its allusion to something lost and to a son had the effect of unravelling some of the threads that bound me to and made up my particular way of suffering. While familiar memories were interpreted differently, new ones emerged and the lost son found its place in the family history.

It is curiously difficult to report something of my own analysis. Curious after all the investment of time, money and much more besides. Curious when surely "my analysis" should be the reply to any question as to why and how I come to spend my working life in the consulting room. Why such inhibition when accounts from analysands – whether fictionalised or not – have proved so helpful in illustrating how psychoanalysis works, or should do or doesn't? The "psychoanalytic" answer is transference. There is, of course, something of a "fall" at the end of those years on the couch, and yet it still seems disloyal, a betrayal of love, to recount the analyst's words said in the privacy their office, and said in a unique way particular to my history, my suffering. So should you, "the analyst" be reading this – sorry and thank you.

Dreams in an Analysis

There are a handful of dreams that stay with me from my analysis, like beacons in a dark sea. The bulk of my analysis has undergone that strange amnesia that befalls a long and completed analysis. These dreams remain with me many years on, condensed and jewel-like, retaining their inherently puzzling quality. Their enduring significance can be explained, firstly, by the forensic interest they appeared to ignite in my analyst; secondly, by the multiple associations that flowed from a single dream, and how words and phrases used in recounting them would pop up in future analytic sessions and dreams; finally, by the interpretations they elicited.

Here I give two abbreviated examples:

The Golden Dog Dream

I was watching my dog (a small black and white terrier) in the distance walking around, but as he came closer, it dawned on me that this was not my dog, and it couldn't be mine as this was a big dog with long golden hair – a bit like Dougal from the Magic Roundabout (a 1970s children's programme).

I became aware of a presence over my left shoulder urging me to accept that this golden dog was my dog. This was not right, and I experienced painful pangs of nostalgia for the loss of my true dog whilst simultaneously accepting that the golden dog was benign, even lovely in its own way and in no way to blame.

Bringing this dream to analysis, I initially associated that the voice over my left shoulder was that of my mother. This came from a memory of a real occasion in which she harangued me from the back seat of a car, albeit over my right shoulder. She was giving me false counsel, not with my best interests at heart. I surmised that maybe the dog in the distance was my partner and the other dog, closer and golden, stood for other men that she'd prefer me to be with.

My analyst asked about 'golden'.

Associations led to my recalling moving at eight years old to California, the 'Golden' State. My mother, sister and I relocated suddenly from the east coast to the west coast of the US, away from living with my father to living with another man. I admitted miserably that I couldn't recall putting up any resistance and,

DOI: 10.4324/9781032637723-21

worse than that, I had even enjoyed living in golden, sunlit, friendly California. Life was easier and had the feel of a perpetual summer holiday.

> My analyst asked me 'What is the colour of gilt?'
> I heard 'What is the colour of guilt?'
> I was plunged into a state of confusion…
> Eventually my analyst offered 'Isn't gilt – g-i-l-t – golden?'.
> Gilt can be applied as a covering of something else.

The dream came to represent my guilt and conflicted feelings at succumbing to the seductive draw of dazzling, golden California and how it's golden sheen had served to cover over and distract me from the reality of leaving my poor, beloved father alone in a grim, wintery place. I recognised that I had always felt complicit in the break-up of my original family.

Dream of the Embodied Lacing

I will describe only a small part of a long and memorable dream produced four years into my analysis, which contained a striking image. This image suits me well as I have a fascination for the macabre.

I am being given a tour by the woman of the house, eccentric, kind but unreliable. Towards the end of a long, varied, and bizarre tour we are in back in the centre of the house with its windows looking out onto an 'amazing rear scene'. She asks me if I would like to come and stay on their Greek island. I accept eagerly. I then become aware of what she is wearing. She is dressed in a Toulouse-Lautrec-style dress with frothy white petticoats, but the dress has a sleazy, faded aura about it, and as she turns around and leans over to write in her diary, I notice a strange division in the back of her dress and that it is gaping open.

With mounting horror, I realise that what I am seeing is the twine of the corsetry sewn through her flesh. The ribbons are laced under her semi-translucent, morbidly white and bloodless flesh which has grown and healed over it.

In a flash, I realise that everything is quite different to how it had seemed to me before. I had been naive and blind to a sinister reality.

The dream associations and interpretations were many, rich and intertwined. For example, in an analytic session more than a year later, my analyst reminded me of the dream of the dress lashed into the back flesh, after I explained that I feared a 'back-lash'. I had been describing indulging in passive-aggressive behaviour towards someone, recognising that I expected, indeed deserved punishment.

I remember at the first telling of the dream that I was leading up to stating, with some embarrassment, what seemed glaringly obvious to me, that the woman in the dress was my analyst. However, as I approached this revelation, my analyst made an interpretation that, in a complete reversal, positioned me as that woman.

It was a vile idea and initially I rejected it, but this interpretation was the start of the ongoing, enigmatic relationship I have with this dream.

This interpretation illustrates for me a hallmark of Lacanian analysis, that of the refusal of the analyst to enter a dual relation with the analysand. Instead of becoming ensnared in an awkward personal association, in this case of being humiliated within my dream, the analyst avoids being trapped through re-direction and/or the invoking of another register.

I made many, often quite sly, attempts to catch my analyst in an imaginary dual relation, and it was an enormous relief when I finally realised that they would never position themselves as a 'little other' to me.

Scenario

I possess an apparently idiosyncratic way of pronouncing the word 'scenario'. I'd uttered the word in a session and my analyst responded with a semi-incredulous 'What?!' I shrugged and thought: 'Well, who can tell you how to say anything?'. It's a moment that's come back to me many times since: who can tell you how to say anything, think anything, do anything, be anything?

My Desk Is Next to My Bed

I went into analysis because I had recently got into a relationship, and I told myself I wanted to give it the best possible chance of working. I had a strong sense that my own particular mode of being was likely to present problems in this regard, and in time I would be proven correct in this assessment. Immediately prior to entering analysis, I had disappeared on a lengthy drinking binge, from which I had returned with cracked ribs and a dislocated toe, injuries sustained during an impromptu wrestling match with a stranger on a deserted beach. During my disappearance, I had made myself uncontactable by my partner, consistently neglecting to contact her, despite feeling wracked by guilt throughout. My promise to enter analysis served as an elaborate *mea culpa* and gesture of earnest intent, or at least I wished for it to.

I was a postgraduate student at the time, although practically in name alone. Upon commencing my analysis, it became apparent to me that my unwillingness to write my thesis was an even weightier preoccupation for me than the risk of real-time relationship sabotage. It would occur to me later that I had been drawn to this relationship because it enabled me to neglect my studies, and that I had entered analysis partly in the hope of protecting this ability. If the relationship failed, I would not be able to go on using it as an excuse to avoid writing. More palpably, my resistance to writing was manifesting itself in the form of an overwhelming urge to get back into bed. This seemed to issue forth whenever I sat down at my desk with the intention of getting some writing done. "My desk is next to my bed", I lamented. My analyst did not respond. As far as I was concerned at the time, in describing the layout of my room, I was drawing attention only to the tantalising proximity of bed to desk. This I felt somehow excused my defeatism. The dimensions of my accommodation were to blame.

At the end of the session, my analyst repeated the phrase back to me: "My desk is next to my bed". Upon reflection, I came to understand this proposition concerning the juxtaposition of the two items of furniture in terms of the somnambulance of my life activity. This was suffused with an urge to sleep, to sedate myself. The sleep in question was nonregenerative, oblivion not rest. I began to perceive its pursuit in my alcoholism, insistent and cunning. I noticed it too in my choice of partner, given to maternalism, sufficiently cruel and unfeeling to foreclose the

DOI: 10.4324/9781032637723-22

possibility of an edifying relationship. I was surrounded by soporific devices. Even worse, I came to realise, this was very much by design.

I had gone back to university ostensibly in order to better myself, having made the decision to do so out of dissatisfaction with my lot: living alone in a caravan in rural Worcestershire, working long hours as a cafe pot-washer. From the perspective of this scenario, further study had presented itself as a zesty enterprise. But three years into my degree, it had become apparent to me that I had effectively sought out refuge in re-institutionalisation. This was an uncomfortable thought. Hearing my analyst repeat the phrase "My desk is next to my bed" back to me reminded me of an aphorism written by the thinker I was failing to write on: "In a dream, I took my life with a gun. When it went off, I did not wake up but saw myself lying for a while as a corpse. Only then did I wake".

Analysis enabled me to see myself lying for a while as a corpse. My thesis was revealed as a shroud, my struggle to write as an agon in bad faith. Conceiving of my life activity as wilfully somnambulant shed new light on the puzzle of my refusal to grasp the nettle and start writing, despite feeling wracked by guilt for neglecting my work. The strength of my desire to go on sleeping was overpowering my nominal commitment to completing my studies. I could not bring myself to finish the task at hand, because its unfinishability was a condition of possibility for its continuing to act as a sedative. Writing my thesis would mean waking up. Firstly, because it is impossible to write somnambulantly, and secondly because graduation stood to rob me of my most plausible soporific device: my extra-mature studentdom. Finishing it would tear off my cover story, the duvet beneath which I slept, non-regeneratively. When I eventually did graduate two years later, I felt intensely miserable.

Seeing myself lying for a while as a corpse made me want to wake up. When I entered analysis, my inability to write was more or less opaque to me. I had been avoiding writing and the problem of my inability to write so studiously that I was not even properly aware of it as a cause of suffering. In time I came to understand my avoidance of writing as the avoidance of an activity that was itself a means of avoiding the question of how to live, of what I wanted to dedicate my life to. Analysis dispossessed me of the ability to sustain my avoidance of this question.

The end of my relationship elicited paroxysms of sadness and intoxication. These I seized upon as a pretext to remove myself from analysis. But the damage to my old way of doing things was done. A year of wilful destruction ensued, at the end of which I committed myself to abstinence from intoxication. Within seven weeks my thesis was complete. I then experimented with new soporific devices, including frenetic industriousness and compulsive holidaymaking. But these were the death rattle of the retreat into a hedonic escapism that had consumed my early thirties, and much of my twenties too.

Random Act

Analysis hinges on entries and exits, the play of presence and absence. Within these variables, a lot happens on the edges, on the boundaries, between sessions, or long after an analysis ends, phenomena most would regard as incidental.

Long before I entered analysis, I came across a delightful book by the American poet Hilda Doolittle recalling her analysis with Freud in the early 1930s. Freud had no qualms discussing matters well outside the usual ken of analytic treatment, including reference to his vast collection of antiquities, which were hard to ignore since they were sprawled across his consulting room. In one significant passage, Doolittle recalls an exchange concerning an antiquity taking pride of place on Freud's desk. A small bronze statute of the Greek goddess Athena, which he proudly declared was his "favourite", stating that this figure was "perfect... only that she has lost her spear". I read a feminist commentary afterwards advocating this was a questionable allusion to female castration, and while Doolittle acknowledged this possibility, she didn't dwell on it, but focused instead on the patent fact the piece was made of bronze as opposed to the classical white of a marble statue. The materiality of the object resonated well beyond the veiled symbolism of Freud's pronouncements. Bronze was a warmer material, she mused, as opposed to the blank coldness of marble. This account possessed an authenticity I thought: while fragmented, it was far more playful than anything I'd read in Freud's case studies. From a poet's perspective surely, it's all between the lines, no clear conclusions can ever be drawn. Something remains unsaid, meaning is left open. There was a generosity to her depiction, Freud had clearly made a lasting impression, but with the distinct sense she'd been left with more questions than answers. Being a retrospective account, written over a decade later, it was clear that her analysis had continued well beyond her short time in Vienna.

A tragic event threw my life into turmoil which urged me to seek an analysis, and over a period of roughly three years, I visited what I now recognise as someone trained in the object-relations tradition. It was containing and supportive, and the metronomic regularity of each session provided a reassuring space to speak. However, if I was ever late, which I sometimes was, it prompted the inevitable response that I must have felt aggrieved or annoyed by something from our previous session. A punitive acting-out perhaps, in response to an unexpected cancellation, an

DOI: 10.4324/9781032637723-23

upcoming break, and invariably conceived as an attack on the therapy. Whilst there was some mileage in exploring such possibilities, it all became rather one dimensional. I found myself rushing, catching earlier trains, clock watching. It signalled a time to move on, or rather, I'd already moved on. It had served a purpose and I'd started speaking.

My second analyst was a Lacanian, who I saw for a number of years over two separate occasions, separated by a gap of seven years. He practiced in London so I had to make a long train journey down from the Midlands. One sunny afternoon, I arrived at our pre-arranged time and pressed the entry buzzer but received no reply. I was quite familiar with waiting for another analysand to finish, so thought no more. After 5 minutes I buzzed again, but still no answer. This was more unusual, normally I would be buzzed in to a waiting area outside his room. Fifteen minutes past the hour, I pressed the bell again, no answer. I gave it one more try 5 minutes later, still no reply. Strangely enough, I didn't feel concerned, this wasn't my mistake and I decided to leave a brief message on his phone. When his answerphone clicked in, I said we had an appointment at 3pm, but it was now 25 minutes past, so I'd booked a train for 5pm and therefore was heading back across the city. Around 3.40pm, the phone rang and my analyst spoke in his distinctive foreign accent. His words seemed heartfelt, "Apologies, I fucked up!". I acknowledged this admission with a laugh and duly thanked him for his honesty. Strangely, after the call a wave of relief crashed over me. It took months to work out why, but I contentedly replayed this scene again and again, obsessively you could say. His words seemed strangely liberating. Mistakes happen, and while it was a big deal, it's wasn't such a big deal. The unsayable can be acknowledged; words help us move on. By giving birth to new meaning something begins to shift.

Many years later, I connected this instance with an interpretation my subsequent analyst offered. Responding to a belief I held as a child that I possessed the mystical power to dissuade my mother from entering any room I was in; my analyst quietly replied, "But surely this was just your way of dealing with the fact she was never going to come in". Her response startled me and slowly forced me to take ownership of my symptom. Keeping things out wasn't an act of choice but merely my reaction to an inevitability.

A persistent blind spot in my practice, a disregard for my patients at key moments, forced me to pick up the gauntlet once again with this third analyst. She worked in London and again it took many hours to reach her consulting rooms. One hot day, I arrived and my analyst greeted me at her door with a glance that acknowledged the distance and asked if I needed a drink. This took me by surprise, yet I replied with a relieved "Yes, thank you". She returned with a glass of orange juice, and while I sat in the waiting room, I found myself weeping as I sipped the cold drink. Analysts don't provide drinks I thought – what happened to analytic reserve and indifference. Yes, it was kind gesture, but what resonated most was the fact she didn't hesitate. My encounter with this act went on to disrupt my entire history, and still does.

A Knock on the Door

I only ever met with one therapist. Years later it is still going, and it has changed my life. I have heard from many people (and known as a therapist myself on the other side of things now) that the luck, the transference, whatever it might be, to allow for such an encounter to lead to productive work is rare.

What have been the moments of analytic interpretation that have changed things? Taking what might count as an act of interpretation widely, I can say what stands out, though I'm not sure how closely remembering an important moment is connected to changes made.

I am in Lacanian analysis. I am not sure if I was at the beginning; certainly I did not seek the Lacanian part out and certain features of its technical practice (for example, the variable length session, cuts to underline important moments) appeared some years in. Some of the peripheral moments have made the strongest mark. It is sometimes said that the moments that happen at the margins of the work, when both patient and therapist are straining under something, are most impactful.

I stayed after the first session because – yes, I was ready to speak to someone and could speak there without construction about things going repeatedly wrong – but what I recall most clearly came after that. I brought no money with me that day. When I asked at the end if I could pay using a card, she said no; I should walk to the nearest card machine and come back. Not such a big thing and yet I felt I'd humiliated myself by not foreseeing this, for the entitlement of not preparing better. Perhaps I did not want to have to pay for this treatment. No interpretation in words was given like this. Rather, she coolly instructed me to go and get the money from a cash point, which I did. A mutual sizing up and an exchange. So I knew I was with someone who would get to the point, and it's been my guiding light of trust ever since.

We began. There have been a few moments like this since then. Requests from me, made without guile. I rushed in one day asking, could she print my essay? I was on my way to hand in an important assignment afterwards, and the high street place I usually used was closed. She looked put out but agreed and then said later, you want me to read it and see how clever you might be. Something like that.

Refusals, demands reframed, have set the stage for me to play things out. In the first year, I made a decision to turn down something I'd been building towards for

DOI: 10.4324/9781032637723-24

years. I finally got a place to study medicine which I turned down, in favour of training to be a therapist. When I got the offer to study medicine, I felt initially gratified then unexpectedly unbearably dreadful: jittery, with racing heart and thoughts. She listened and asked questions and challenged unexamined ideas in such a way that I was able to think critically and make that decision without ever sensing an opinion from her.

About two years in, I worked as a live-in nanny outside London for a few months, and I wondered if this would be a problem – not being able to attend sessions in person as usual. To my surprise, she encouraged me to take the job, suggesting it could function a bit like an infant observation (a key part of some therapy trainings, though not mine).

That summer while looking after a three-year-old and a new born baby, I texted my analyst before my working day began at 6:30 am, and she then called me to initiate each session. The way I remember it, I barely spoke for weeks on end. We both woke up early, but I spoke very few words. Sometimes I cried and at the end of the session, she would say, 'Our next session is on...' Even the configuration of my text – in effect a 'knock on the door' to her and her then calling me, inviting me to speak with her desire to listen – I ignored at the time. In retrospect it seems thoughtful: it made me reaffirm my desire to speak each time. I felt very attached to her during this period and being far away was difficult. The children I was looking after were sweet, the family kind and the dynamics interesting. I enjoyed it but I also found the long days of solo childcare lonely and boring. It was a new experience to be in charge of the older girl all day whose relationship with her mother had just been profoundly altered by the birth of a sibling and the death of her mother's mother. There was a lot swimming in my unconscious. I seemed to be in contact with something quite deadened and impassable at this point in my therapy, noticing their early childhood bonds, and the immersion in this rendered me silent.

It was frustrating, probably for us both, but she tolerated it and helped me do the same. There were no interpretations of my fraught silences, only requests for what I was thinking, delineating patiently for me that there is a difference between thinking nothing and having nothing to address to another person for their sake. It remains an open space for me, that time.

Of course, there have been recurrent classical interpretations made, rejected and remade that are what we might call more classical interpretations associated with analysis: Oedipal tangles with parental figures and partners. These have been important and relate to the issues I sought therapy for in more explicit, content-based ways, but seeing where interpretations have been made and where I have been put to work in interpreting things myself has I think made this a longer lasting process.

The features that feel more Lacanian to me (the short sessions, the careful attention to language) do what any decent interpretation might: they make me think about what I've said. Having someone ask you with grave interest to repeat a word mumbled carelessly one day and then tap their fingers in theatrical impatience the next, presumably because it feels to them as if you're just 'chatting', makes you listen to yourself and think in a new way. The attention paid to my words, and in them the unconscious at work, is something I associate with Lacanian analysis. The woman I see takes her work very seriously but she is also witty and humorous. I think this has something to do with Lacanian theatre and acts of interpretation being carefully chosen to put words to work.

Betrayal

In the early stages of my analysis, my analyst made an interpretation through the introduction of a word: "betrayal". It was used to describe an act of my mother's, which I had, until that point, rationalised into a matter-of-fact. A fact, I could say, that did not impinge on me in any way: I understood my mother's position, I empathised with it.

This "betrayal" was then used by my analyst to refer to multifarious points in my history, which worked to reframe them and to tie them together. It worked, in other words, to reconfigure my history implicating my mother in so many of its twists and turns. It provided an opening towards seeing anew the seemingly inexplicable encounters I kept finding myself in.

I did not take to this interpretation immediately, and, in some ways, I still hold my reservations about it: such an interpretation is blinkered, unable to encompass the subtleties of my familial experience. But it is precisely for this reason that it was so useful: it worked to "tighten" my history through making links not hitherto made, which, in turn, allowed new perspectives to unfold.

Ultimately, something was unstuck. Over time, this interpretation has allowed a further separation from my mother, from her history and desire, or, put another way, from her terms of understanding that were unconsciously mine.

DOI: 10.4324/9781032637723-25

Grampy

I want to speak about a dream late in the life of a psychoanalyst, a product of self-analysis, that delimits the incestuous familial field and establishes the difference between the generations through the figure of the analyst and the place of the analyst's desire. It shows something critical about the work of an analyst's analysis and a question about the field itself. The dream began with the phrase "Psychoanalysis has forgotten the world, and the world has forgotten psychoanalysis," which was in the context of the attempt to build a transatlantic tunnel that couldn't be completed. A kind of melancholic statement of negation and forgetting, close to Freud's "I don't love him, I don't love anyone, I love only myself."

Recently, I had been in the subway with my son in another city, and we had marvelled at their train stations' round structure. I spoke with him about how subways all look different in different cities. We talked about how fun it must be for a city to decide on the architectural aesthetics of their subway system.

After catching a glimpse of this half-completed tunnel, the scene changed to a thrift store, where a friend was showing me old miniature paintings by masters, which seemed to cost and be worth hundreds of thousands of dollars. I had the desire to steal one but resisted. After having taken the back off one to examine the construction of the painting, perhaps to assess whether it was real, the painting got lost in the shuffle. I was only left with the frame. I was terrified that I wouldn't be able to prove my innocence if caught, since I had in fact wanted to steal it, but then I began to doubt myself. Had I in fact stolen it?

The scene changes again, and I am with my stepmother. It is revealed that she has been stealing money from my father, that they live quite separately, and that he was in fact quite alone, as she lives elsewhere. Suddenly, I am being told that my father has died and that I must go to the hospital to make arrangements; but the term used is "grampy," or what my son calls my father, and it is now my father telling me. It is as if he has split into two people, father/grampy. I am told that I have inherited an office that I can use for my psychoanalytic practice, but when I go to visit this office (and not my dead father), my second analyst (who bears my father's mother's name) is the person who runs the building. I wonder if this is an appropriate arrangement, and the dream ends.

DOI: 10.4324/9781032637723-26

When I woke up, I realized that the "proper" Oedipal parental couple had been created by the dream—Grampy and my analyst—a couple I never knew, since my father's father had died tragically when my father was a child. In fact, my mother's father also died tragically when my mother was a child—probably the real reason they married each other, this problem with the loss of fathers—so I never had a grandfather. My mother's mother never remarried and raised eight children alone. My father's mother remarried, but this husband also died suddenly not long after they were married and she never remarried. My parents, after they divorced, married younger spouses that never had children, and so one could say that there was never an intact family: a fact of my heritage, but one also linked to historical condition of Depression, immigration, and war.

In creating the lost parents of my parents through my analyst, the dream points to the destruction of the family, from which my parents never recovered and from which I, in some ways, also have not. The figure of the analyst who holds the lineage is meant to dispel guilt. I want to steal as if there is something to take, against a whole field of impossible losses that mark the generations.

This points to a line of transgression reminiscent of Freud's father in his experience at the Acropolis, who says to him, "Be where I am and go no further." This signaling fuels the wish, the prohibition, and its place in a family-romance fantasy. This dream comes at a moment when I want to cross the line, steal what isn't supposed to belong to me, and was having great difficulty without knowing why. The dream starts incompletely, moves to a lack and a sense of not understanding a scene of guilt, and then finally marks the boundary between generations.

My mother lost a child late in a pregnancy, something that marked my birth, her abandonment of me, and the disintegration of my parent's marriage. More than this, her blame—of my father, of me—was already a displaced reaction and repetition in relation to the loss of her own father. My father's helplessness in the face of women is part of his own repetition—left to take care of his mother whose husbands kept dying. An unconscious economy of blame circulates as the melancholic family bond. This is how families are destroyed. All of this is as it is.

It's funny that the dream is set off by this strange pronouncement about the psychoanalytic institution. God knows I am no fan of it, and I quickly saw through the family romance of the institution itself, even when I was seduced by it. The recognition of its shattered state, compassion for what is so impossible about an institution for psychoanalysis, seemed necessary for me to find my way out of what was so disappointing. But the truth is also valuable for psychoanalysis to figure out how to be relevant again in a world that hasn't just turned against it, as they often like to imagine, but had completely forgotten it—something that seemed impossible to know if they held close to *their* romance with which they unethically seduced candidates as if they were the center of the world. Be displaced. Acknowledge what has been torn asunder.

I am some generational anomaly, the product of an incomplete transatlantic tunnel. In a way, I knew and acted on all this first and left the psychoanalytic institutional fold before I knew the entrenched place of "all of it" in my own life, in relation to my family history. Knew is an overstatement, I knew some; I know some now. This dream, on the other hand, crystallized something, perhaps not because of this alliance between my history and my formation as an analyst, but because of working as an analyst. This is the frame that I must work with.

Psychoanalysis probably forgot the world in its own melancholy, caught in two World Wars and its history of infighting, gossip, and blame is sad when it's not untoward. But the story isn't extraordinary. It is, in some sense, common—as common as a miscarriage, a divorce, a death, war, and displacement, immigration— even if it sounds like the fated stories psychoanalysts like to tell. I don't think I like telling it. We must move on.

'Analysis Terminable and Interminable', Thirty Years On

Preamble

The invitation to write about a special moment in my analysis may well have been an instance of 'synchronicity'. Thirty years after my initial Lacanian analysis, I had just started a private practice and was re-engaging with psychoanalysis at a deeper level, when it came through.

Initially, I ignored the invitation, declined it even, feeling unwilling to revisit and evaluate three decades of my life. However, the response I got back piqued my curiosity and pointed to the possible revelations such an endeavour could unmask. It read:

> ...your contribution would have been so intriguing – given your stance, no problem at all, I understand!

My stance being that after three decades I could no longer remember the fine grain of my analysis, the 'special moments'. I could only remember general impressions to do with factors common across all psychotherapeutic interventions...

My reaction, of curiosity, reflection, and eventual engagement, strikes me like that of a psychoanalytic intervention and has clarified for me how the psychoanalytic process can work. Its non-judgemental, interested, interesting and intriguing, 'mirroring back' of the words spoken elicits curiosity and stokes up the courage to articulate and follow through the most ephemeral of thoughts, snatches of speech, syllables, fragments of dreams, feelings, memory lapses, etc. It does not simply answer a demand for relief from symptoms – and to collude with a person's settled, but pernicious way of being in the world (something more appropriate to counselling maybe) – but creates instead an attitude of enquiry which can no longer take anything for granted, especially oneself and one's chosen lifestyle.

Shortly after accepting, I was able to remember (of course) a particularly graphic intervention, one which condensed and combined several unacknowledged themes in my life at the time. My analyst simply asked:

> Why don't you f*** books instead?

DOI: 10.4324/9781032637723-27

In Retrospect

One theme was my relationship to books. Books of Fiction had always been my friends, especially when I was at boarding school. Study books, however, were a different matter; I would very soon become fidgety and restless, unless that is the subject matter fired my passion. Like when my English literature A level teacher first introduced me to Freudian theory and got me hooked on psychoanalysis in the form of psychoanalytic literary criticism, to explain, for example, 'Macbeth's' tragic self-destruction or the wilderness lurking in many of us, as revealed by 'Lord of the Flies'.

My problem was that due to my 'family myth' of heroic men (my three uncles had been 'heroes' of the French 'Resistance', and my father a jungle veteran of the 'Malayan Emergency' 1948–1960), I had a love of physical prowess, shining on the sports field, and never shy of backing down from physical confrontation. This meant that I dealt with social situations physically, and I released tension physically and later sexually. I thus found it hard to stay with frustration and persevere through it.

This proved extremely challenging when training with Centre for Freudian Analysis and Research (CFAR). For as well as the above, my family culture had been rural rather than metropolitan, and the Parisian intellectual culture I saw Lacan as embodying seemed artificial, elitist, and deliberately obfuscating. Although I was a native French speaker, I hated the frustratingly impenetrable 'Lacanese' (although I was aware of the explanations or rather, as I thought at the time, the rationalisations for it). My memory of training as well as my analysis was one of mainly feeling frustrated and angry, which nevertheless was handled by my analyst so as not to curtail my burgeoning curiosity and my dawning apprehension of what I really wanted: meaning, purpose, a better fitting identity, and an ability to work and to love. And learning to bear inevitable frustration by seeking understanding rather than immediate physical displacement or release.

Another theme was sex of course, so that at the time of the intervention, I was lurching from relationship to relationship, sometimes monogamously, sometimes not.

Unfortunately, I cannot remember the immediate effects of my analysts' words and my specific reactions to it. But I do know that it occurred in the first or second year of my 11-year-long analysis, that, somehow, I was able to persevere with the training, reading introductory texts on Lacan (some notable for their exceptional clarity), as well as a lot of Freud. I went on to practice 'psychoanalytic psychotherapy' in the charitable and Nation Health Service (NHS) contexts for 25 years, very much influenced by Lacanian practice. I also survived a divorce without too much damage and did eventually follow my desire to raise a family.

Epilogue

Looking back, it is clear that my analyst's graphic intervention was monumental in its effects and that it was an injunction to 'sublimate' – channel and transform my sexual and aggressive energies into committing to that youthful passion for psychoanalysis, first awakened in me at school (but later laid aside at the University for the clearer and more promising prospects of a career in Psychology, which I didn't enjoy), and to gain and acquire the knowledge and experience I needed to do that.

There is so much more to say really, like the different phases of analysis, and how towards the end I realized that I would always have challenges but that I would be able to face them, as indeed I did when my father died, and when for a while all meaning drained from the world.

How through my exposure to other modes of psychotherapy in the NHS I noted that although their symptom management techniques were useful for some people in the short term, the benefits seemed to wither away with time. In my newly established private practice, I have been surprised by how many people seeking psychoanalysis have tried these other interventions already.

When I first lay on my analyst's couch all those years ago, I said, 'Ah somewhere I can tell my lies', and she responded, 'Yes, if you want'. In the spirit, I believe, of acknowledging that these inevitably wove the web from which deeper truths could emerge. I hope that the recollections I have laid down here, undoubtedly suffused by different time frames, wishful thinking, idealisation, knowledge, and insights gained over 30 years, will be taken in that same spirit.

The gift of psychoanalysis, it seems to me, is that it liberates within us and hopefully others, an uncommon or even 'holy' curiosity which can be a self-sustaining source of insight, new meaning, and rejuvenation in the face of new challenges. In this sense, psychoanalysis thankfully is truly 'interminable'.

Less than Zero

About a year in I entered my analyst's room uncharacteristically sure about what I wanted to speak about. My partner had expressed the desire for us to go away for a few weeks to another continent, and I was eager to explain to my analyst why it did not make sense to go. I began to speak: 'It will cost loads of money, the flights will cost £1000, and when we are there it will cost about £2,000 minimum. I only have £5,000 in the bank, if I go I will basically be back on zero', 'Back?' my analyst asked, to which I instantly responded with the words 'Yes I've pretty much lived my life on zero'. She smiled and said 'Okay' before walking me out the door.

As I walked down the street, I felt immediately lighter, excited even. Inexplicably I found myself looking forward to the possibility of the trip and at that moment recorded a message to my partner saying that I thought that we should go and made some suggestions of how we could save some cash to put towards it.

I have little real understanding of why I said those words in the session, what they mean, or why my analyst chose to stop the session there after what had been only about a minute. What is miraculous to me is that an immediate change had occurred, my position had shifted. It is not simply that I went from No to Yes about the holiday, but that since then my relationship towards spending money, making decisions, my partner's desire, commitment, and thinking about the future have all radically changed, so much so that the best way I can describe the effect of this moment is 'freedom'.

DOI: 10.4324/9781032637723-28

A Love Letter

I met my analyst shortly after moving to Paris, on a friend's recommendation, as someone who'd been working on my topics of interest. I began to attend his seminar, which I enjoyed despite my pitiful French; when I was ready to start analysis some months later, I realised my choice of analyst had already been made.

Thinking of what "worked" in my analysis, a moment came to mind from this very first period of analysis, perhaps only weeks after its beginning. At the end of a session, I was surprised to find that I was exactly ten Euro short of the agreed fee. I apologised and promised to bring the missing cash the following time. However, on leaving I realised this was the day of the seminar. I didn't have to wait! In the evening, I put a ten Euro note in an envelope and, during the break, I walked up to my analyst and presented him with this "letter" with a meaningful look. A feeling of relief and satisfaction (I was able to repay the debt sooner than expected and thus restore my status as a model patient!) suddenly turned into panic when I saw his puzzled expression and the bemused looks of his colleagues.

Without missing a beat, my analyst took the envelope from me, briefly peered in, made a somewhat theatrical "Ah!" sound and, with a smile, put the letter in his pocket. But for me, the damage was done, and I fled the room utterly mortified. What I thought had been a simple monetary exchange in fact gave rise to a gesture that, in a manner quite uncharacteristic of my usually shy presence, communicated much more than I'd been prepared to say, bringing to mind aspects of my childhood and romantic history I'd previously been carefully keeping to myself.

Since then, I've come to see this feeling of deep embarrassment – which briefly made me consider abandoning the analytical endeavour altogether, just as it had started – as the hallmark of the unconscious. Anxiety may not deceive, as Lacan would have it, but nothing quite beats the feeling of having your nose shoved deep in your own symptom. One could argue that the connection between the public and private scenes of the seminar and the consulting room, which in my case, given certain elements of my history, facilitated this acting-out, is a legacy of Lacan's own personal style and in this sense unique to Lacanian analysis, contrary to a more Anglo-Saxon interpretation of the analytical principles of neutrality and abstinence. It is well known that Lacan did not shy away from using his position as a teacher to manipulate the transference of his analysands, many of whom attended

DOI: 10.4324/9781032637723-29

his seminar and sometimes felt personally addressed by his various articulations. It is, of course, difficult to judge just how intentional these machinations really were: perhaps, as in my case, the unconscious material simply made use of the tension between the two scenes. However, their occurrence also illustrates Lacan's idea of transference as a love for someone presumed to know, to know something about one's own subjective truth, so that on occasion their mere presence may provoke effects that, on the condition of finding a place of address, can lead to an elaboration.

Gay Shame, Phantasy and Recovering Myself

Through reflections and the clarity that my analysis gifted me, I have come to accept that had matters gone well for me, my own unique sensibility as a young boy would have led me to ultimately identify and be content as a cis gay man.

However, two major social coercions influenced and impacted me. The first has been a fairly universal force in all children, patriarchy, and the second, it's convenient bedfellow: heteronormativity. One could view these as perverse symbolic laws projected through society, culture and religion.

Perhaps far more significant for me though was in the realm of unconscious phantasy, this being far less accessible and ultimately imprisoning.

By my early 20s, my innocent and largely unproblematic same-sex explorations began to form a tightening noose around my neck. Always a sensitive child and unbeknown to me, I had taken up an incestual imaginary position in relation to both the desire of my father and mother seeking their approval and endorsement in most areas. Incestual because of the gratification and cosiness it brought unconsciously, problematic in that it prevented me from recognising my own free subjective desire. I instead insisted on remaining fused to this ultimately destructive position and refusing my own potential, facilitated through a necessary sense of lack, deliverable through the disruptiveness of a symbolic law (a NO!). The loss of my omnipotent, narcissistic gratifications was to be prevented at all costs, instead maintaining an ultimately painful entrapment and death drive, like a 'moth to a flame'.

I modelled my captivity around their subtle judgements of homosexuality, particularly during the very visual and catastrophic AIDS epidemic at that time. Their desire for me to become a 'professional' and marry a good girl would validate their immigration aspirations and thus satisfy me as a 'job done' for them. Unknowingly for me and yet tragically for those impacted around me (my future wife in particular), being their 'object of desire' became my *raison d'etre*.

At its height, and although consciously very content with my life, I was gaining huge gratification in being the 'all giving' son, husband and father. Gradually, however, over the next 25 years, I began to suffer from increasing obsessive compulsive symptoms which I would often frame as a sort of joke within my family, to hide their severity and impact on me. There was an emergence of anxiety too in the form of resurfacing same-sex fantasies, kept at bay for many years. Catastrophic

DOI: 10.4324/9781032637723-30

fears suffocated me that if I ever indulged my growing thoughts of being with men, I would infect both myself and my wife with HIV. The punishing masochism was a very neat, convenient and complex knot. This all proved to be a volatile tinder that would ignite in the months ahead.

To truly understand the level of unconscious repression at play, even a five-year twice weekly training therapy to become a psychotherapist myself did not truly bring to light my unconscious suffering. My delusional ability was so sophisticated at this time that I accepted my sexuality by only recognising it as a 'bi curiosity', something that I could tame or consciously deny myself. I reflect on it now like a chronically blocked sewage system that allows only a trickle of waste to pass through.

My supervisor made certain observations in my clinical work. Something just didn't seem balanced in me finding my voice with my clients. I accepted that my obsessional symptoms and anxiety clearly indicated to me a need to return to therapy myself, but this time I sought the assistance of a Lacanian psychoanalyst.

'Why have you come?'

The very careful and specific attention given to the construction of my thoughts, phantasies and dream recollections was quite different to what I had previously encountered. I had complex feelings of being incredibly exposed with no here to hide. There was much compassion in the work but no indulgence given to any comfort or cosiness in the physical or psychic space. My sessions were repeatedly 'cut' when my unconscious briefly opened like an unravelling rose bud. To take advantage of these moments of lucidity, I'd be told to return after a short walk or later in the day. I was constantly called to account. It was brutal yet exhilarating. 'What was the worst thing you could have done to your mother?' 'To have been a gay man': cut. HIV and AIDS became a 'lethal' signifier of my jouissance. The falling 'AIDS tombstone' in a TV public safety announcement watched with my parents, and their subsequent comments were sealed in a language vault with them as my Big Others.

I attended for a few short months only, often three to four times over the same weekend whilst my analyst was visiting London from Paris. One time I walked out, completely frustrated and still in denial, refusing to accept what I knew was around the corner. 'When will you stop this suffering?' I was told. The day I accepted the full extent of my delusional constructions, I wept with him like never before. 'Now you have accepted what you have done to yourself and what you are, you have some difficult choices'. From that day forward, although incredibly concerned at the thought of the road ahead, I felt like a light had switched on in me. It sounds very cliched, but I see it as my subjective truth. Such clarity had never existed for me. It was devastating in the aloneness that it brought at that time, but it allowed me an agency that I'd never perceived possible. My life was to unravel but the light would never extinguish.

One of the first things that I recall was the immediate withdrawal of my obsessional symptoms. I still had immense concerns and worries, but I was no longer catastrophically anxious. Tragically, I was no longer able to feel remotely sexually engaged with my wife. I have come to accept that my ability to have sex over the years with this wonderful woman who I lost my virginity to was founded predominantly on immense love and hope. Just like the surgeon who inverts his gloves after a long and successful operation, they just cannot be replaced in the same way. I was permanently changed. I have no bisexual attraction. Within weeks I had spoken to my wife first and then to my children. As one can only imagine, it continues to be a difficult journey at times. However, with love and huge respect, my relationship with my now ex-wife is gradually being re-symbolised, but my children have been magnificent anchors. Our Titanic certainly hit an immense iceberg, but rather than sink, we have managed to reach a place of safety as a family.

There was no recognisable relationship with my analyst. Once the work was done, it was over. I still see him occasionally in an academic setting. He has asked me at times informally how I am. I reply simply and hope he is aware of how indebted I am to the work we undertook. My analysis was the truest of ethical encounters for me. It was incredibly hard but it simply had to be.

The Goodbye

One simple interpretation of my analyst worked to relive me from the oppressive remorse and guilt I was feeling for not being able to give a last goodbye to a dear person to me when she was in a coma. What had happened was that I had been phoned and asked if I wished to travel there for a last goodbye. I thanked them but said I could not get a flight at that moment.

"The goodbye was for you, not for your beloved" was the comment of the analyst. That simple intervention has been very helpful, distancing me from the guilt and helping me to move on, starting to elaborate that loss.

DOI: 10.4324/9781032637723-31

Samson and Delilah

"Life as a commentary on something else we cannot reach, which is there within reach of the leap we will not take.

Life, a ballet based upon a historical theme, a story based upon a deed that once had been alive, a deed that had lived based upon a real deed." (Cortazar, p. 448)

The most instigating moments in my analysis were those that presented me with a sense of an opening beyond what had been said, but in a not very clear way of what that entailed. A sort of leap or new meaning would tease out new paths to elaborate. This movement could be felt as an effort to run towards something while running away from it at the same time. The urge to jump into the next train of associations and not knowing clearly what I was doing was somehow crucial to be able to make use of that process.

To recall a specific example, I will bring up the effect of a comment about how I had developed a style, having produced a number of developments in my analysis. The most immediate effect was that through this term I was then able to circumscribe my mode of being as a way of getting by, which consisted of some sort of hiding. By bringing together the idea of representing and masking through fitting into a format, I focused on moments in which this featured strongly in my life.

The next associations around style were linked to memories of the time I became more accepting of a more traditional feminine identity. I remembered how a lot of my references from the age of eight were from old movies I used to watch every week with my grandmother. She especially loved films from the 40s and 50s, and these references populated my imagination throughout my childhood, allowing me to create an image to go by, to emulate. An important aspect to that particular aesthetic was that it was no longer present around me, and these references were largely not shared by my peers. The anachronism was essential, as it brought with it a sense of inaccessibility and nostalgia. I became aware through these memories that although I found in cinema a form of inclusion and representation, the element of discontinuity and unfamiliarity brought by it was also desirable. It was a way of inclusion but also exclusion.

A third wave of associations that was ignited by the idea of a style took me to my childhood mythology. Around the age of four years old, I developed an interest in Samson and Delilah's story. The idea of a man so strong becoming feeble and

DOI: 10.4324/9781032637723-32

pitiful seemed to be my main focus and preoccupation. Around this was also the sense that power may lie in something easy to lose, like one's hair. Most perplexing was Delilah's intentions. Why would she have wanted to do that to Samson?

Through this highlighting of how the theme of style had organised my past, my efforts at mimetic identifications at this time became clear. I wanted to be physically strong, especially to compete with boys at school and wished to be considered one of them, although feeling I was something else. This somehow resembled the function cinema had later on for me, producing an identification but inevitably also a gap, a distancing. Looking back, the very focus on Samson and Delilah was already a somewhat interpretative attempt to make sense of my struggles around power, gender and identity. Through the fixation on this story, I seemed to be giving body to something that hadn't been able to be represented.

Perhaps the psychoanalytical interpretation I found most helpful was more on the side of Delilah's action, an undoing of some arrestingly powerful image through the wrecking of a sign, creating a gap in an identification, having it functioning more on the side of resonances and movement than of precision and identity. By necessity, time and events challenge the image to a point it becomes unsustainable in a permanent manner. There could have been, in my attempts to create associations, a wish for a sparkle of an identity that would not be sustainable in a more lasting way. A constant working through of representations that by testing the limits of what they propose sustains a tension between belonging and longing to be.

Bibliography

Cortazar, J. (2020). *Hopscotch*. London: Vintage.

What's in a Name?

Trudging uphill in a bazaar, where merchants offer their wares, I weave between market-oers, chasing after a small child, who in turn morphs into...my mother? I finally catch up at the top of the hill next to the final stall, where a fishmonger is standing. Suddenly, dressed for a day at the office, I wait as he unfurls a rolled-up eel and presents it to me as like a diploma. Eel? Asks my analyst. Eel...Lee...my middle name and my maternal grandfather's middle name. He was the first to get a Master's degree and become a credentialed professional.

Years later, pregnant for the second time, I dream of a new name:

At the theatre waiting to see a concert. I paid for tickets in advance, maybe too early, and now wait, observing those who are buying their tickets then and there and somehow getting escorted to better seats. I look around at who I've brought with me. My husband. My son. I whisper to my husband with a chuckle, "I'm changing my name to Hortensia."

In recounting this dream to my analyst, the associations pour forth: *Hortensia*? *Hortense*? Whore-tense? During my first labour, my cervix did not dilate. Anxiety rises as I approach the due date for this second child. This part of my anatomy holds past trauma, scars from an early, precocious sexuality. These marks of pain from the past cause me to brace and hold myself tight in the present. Hearing "Whore-tense" in this name conjured by my unconscious leads again to a laugh, a release. I move on in a new direction. *Hortense* is a French name meaning "gardener." *Hortensia* is the common name for one of my favourite summer blossoms, hydrangeas.

An assumption of names, old and new at these moments of symbolic transformation—the first, stepping into a place in a professional world that had long felt barred, a question of how to find and make my own mark, my own work; the second, at a moment of recognition of ever-becoming. The first dream bears a phallic element, as I earn the male name already bestowed upon me. In the second dream, which arrives decades later, in another chapter of analysis, driven by the desire to be an analyst myself, the name arrives through a joke, a production of my own unconscious and its relation to the many-petaled feminine. It is a name that moves through time, desires, and the real of my body. It is a name that embodies

DOI: 10.4324/9781032637723-33

a reckless past with bawdy humour and a nod to what has become of that libidinal force, something I cultivate and tend to in my role as a mother and in my work as an analyst, listening for the signifiers that hold the potential to mark the past tense in the present and let it flower toward the future.

The Choice of Exile

I was born in a country that invented the expression *carne de divan*, "couch meat", to designate presumed candidates for analysis from adolescence. It's an expression we use among friends. It is not an insult; it is both a gentle mockery and also an encouragement for the other to deal with their problems.

We thus identify in everyday language people who may be sufficiently tormented by existence, wondering about life, conflicts, questions about the confusion of love, desire and enjoyment.

I did not belong to this category, at least that's what I believed. I was destined for medical studies which I was able to complete without difficulty, except that a significant experience would determine my future: a year spent abroad for reasons of my choice.

I said it, I continued my studies without a hitch except… that I was seeing someone, as we said, for a while, to talk about a romantic contingency.

I then learned that this someone was a psychoanalyst. The beneficial nature of these meetings had marked me enough, so that when it was time to make my choice of specialty, psychiatry, I asked to see him again. This time, I asked for an analysis and I learned at that time that he said he was Lacanian, which meant nothing to me. When formulating my request for analysis, I announced: "It is for training purposes. I cannot imagine being a psychiatrist without doing an analysis."

How great was my surprise to see how my whole life was turned upside down as the masks were lifted that the phrase "for training purposes" had hidden! The second surprise was that after a certain period of analysis, my analyst left the country. This time I looked for another analyst, and my request was for a Lacanian analyst not "for training purposes" but because once I lifted the lid, I wanted to know more.

Nevertheless, a question bothered me: what is a Lacanian analyst? I was sure that Lacan had to be experienced. From then on, I knew that by staying in my country, I was going to miss a fundamental dimension of the analytic experience. Indeed, no one had yet done an analysis with Lacan.

This is how I decided to come to France. It took me a while to realize that my request for analysis was an alibi. It was hiding what really concerned me. Gradually I realized that my anxieties, my inhibitions and my symptoms covered hidden

DOI: 10.4324/9781032637723-34

desires: those that I had not had the courage to admit to myself, because I had thought they were impossible to achieve.

Strictly speaking, I could testify that this journey resulted above all in a reconciliation with the desires of a child who had remained crushed to satisfy the desire of the Other. What is also certain is that without these analyses, I would not have been able to come to France.

This is where the desire for analysis met a suspended desire, which I evoked at the start, which involved a long stay in a country far from that of my origins, when I had not yet finished high school. I went to this meeting.

So, I resumed my analysis in France, and it was there that I was able to notice the first difference with the previous analyses, especially since each session, each word, was of capital importance. Certainly, the principle of free association was the same – speak, say what comes into your mind – but a further requirement was present from the first moment until the last. To speak was to aim for the unspeakable, beyond what I had always been able to say, so that each session contained something new. I was able to begin to feel that facing the absolute risk of an unheard-of speech had consequences. A desire began to emerge, one that combines psychoanalysis and exile. Dealing with psychoanalysis could justify an exile. The question ran through this last part of the analysis. Can one lose one's country, renounce what was marked as one's own destiny?

Admittedly, in the meantime there were the contingencies of life that tipped the scales in favour of exile. But these contingencies were also the rendezvous to which my unconscious had led me. This is where the dimension of an absolute risk takes on its full meaning, that is, not calculable, which leaves the door wide open to the unexpected. Tearing myself away from my country and my language to answer the enigma of what a Lacanian analyst is seemed to me sufficient reasons to do so. However, I had to see through analysis the many circuits hidden by the certainty of my decision.

However, an interpretation from my second analyst was enough for me to grasp my position. Being told "Lacan does not need to be defended" made me see the distance between defending the person and supporting a theory. My certainty hid the impasses of my training.

So, I dropped into the treatment, the fight to support Lacan, to appropriate his theoretical orientation. As far as I am concerned, the analysis took place in two languages. First of all, in my mother tongue with the three analysts I met. It was the common mother tongue with my first two analysts. Then, in Paris, you needed an analyst who spoke the same language, although it wasn't common, because I didn't speak enough French to do an analysis.

I had been warned. "Do your analysis with someone who has the same mother tongue as you because the end of the analysis presupposes sharing with the analyst the imperatives inscribed by the superego." Yet I was convinced that the idea of necessarily doing an analysis with an analyst of the same mother tongue was a prejudice. During the last part of my analysis – and for some time – my dreams were in French and determined the language of the analysis right up until the end.

Switching to French was essential. No doubt there was a transferential dimension, but after a while this switch became a vital necessity. I can't say that I chose to do it. It had become obvious. Regarding the end, I realized that what emerged as unique in language was not shareable, not understandable, and it was necessary to bear testimony to this.

No Parents!

More than an interpretation it was a statement: 'You did not have any parents!'

Before my Lacanian analyst pronounced herself on the non-existence of my parents' parental function, I had thought of them as bad parents. Quite suddenly I was catapulted into the world as parentless…I had never imagined such a thing, though the truth of it did hit me straight, the unmissable power of words. I looked back on my life of about 40 years and realised that I had spent a lot of time searching for parents; new parents; good parents; clever ones; giving ones; parents who would hold me in mind; parents who would be models to emulate; parents who could tell me to grow up, to man up and not to be so silly; and parents I would call on for comfort, to talk.

And mainly I looked up to psychoanalysts to fill that vacant place. Why I did so is very simple to understand: at 14 I had an eccentric literature teacher who showed surprise at the class for not having read Freud yet. What else was there to do then but go and read Freud?

It was not the whole story. If it had been, I most likely would not be able to tell the tale, and I would have been in serious trouble. I was in serious trouble nevertheless, sort of.

My parents' emotional absence was partially plugged by the presence of my nanny who took care of us (I had a brother) from the word go…a loving woman who chain-smoked in the nursery, read novels compulsively and had no other concern but us.

She died when I was 12 and is idealised to this day.

The shift from bad parents to no parents meant a huge gap had opened up: no back up, no shouldering, no ramp to lean on. Strangely I had been leaning on my bad parents. I had a complaint which had shaped me (though I was saying that the only thing you couldn't do was to complain!). The memories of blows my mother had delivered to me quite innocently allowed me to forget my absent father and go on and on at my analysts. I did it with the passion of a hurt woman I was myself re-hurting repeatedly through engaging in destructive activities. I was demonstrating a 'look what you've done to me', with a masochism which kept its name hidden.

DOI: 10.4324/9781032637723-35

Having to review and reconstruct my life without parents did calm me down. I accepted that there was no common measure between someone who had had the support of their family and someone who had not had it. This could not be altered. What could be altered was my many attempts to obtain what I felt deeply entitled to. Only then could the screaming void be neutralised...

A Cut Off

A personal experience of the imaginary in my own analysis was a time when I was talking of something of concern to my analyst where I was earnestly explaining a difficulty that I was experiencing. It felt very important that I talked to him, which on this occasion was over the phone. My analyst was particularly quiet in this session until I realised after what seemed a long time that we had been cut off. On calling him back, I said "we were cut off" to which he responded "I know".

I had no desire to repeat what I had been talking about over what seemed like a long time, but possibly about 5 minutes. However, I realised that imagining he had been listening to me on the other end of the phone had been enough, the fact that he hadn't seemed irrelevant.

DOI: 10.4324/9781032637723-36

"Mmms"

When I started analysis, as in the popular trope, I assumed there would eventually come – after months or years – a life-changing interpretation, the moment when everything falls into place as the analyst reveals what's at the root of it all. I don't think that happened – or maybe I didn't either listen or hear, even though I thought I was eager for her every word. I don't remember much at all of what she said in the first year or so as I talked and talked about something I needed to get off my chest until I was all talked out.

My analyst made many helpful interpretations; to give an example, she pointed out that the biggest family arguments I described had happened at points of separation – this enabled me to see how painful it was for my mother (and me) to let go. This was a significant re-framing, a change of perspective on what I sort of already knew. Maybe not life-changing, but many such interventions together added up to a clearer view, a falling into place of scenes from the past. She had an exhaustive range of 'Mmms', in which I heard everything from 'Absolutely!' to 'Really?!' to 'Oh dear...' and so much more. These were sometimes supportive and empathic, but at other times were not the 'Mmm' I was expecting – especially when there came a '???' – and this was all it took to suggest there might be another way of looking at things. These were thousands of mini-interpretations over the years, and I couldn't even say how I calibrated or moulded myself in response.

All of the 'Mmms' together offered an essential recognition, but because my analyst was vivacious and engaged – far from the cryptic chin-stroker – her silence, when she used it, was powerful. When the expected 'Mmmm' didn't come and I couldn't see her expression, I was left hanging, wondering what she thought and, since I wanted her good opinion, whether I had said something dreadful. It's challenging to expose your innermost thoughts and not be reassured in some way – not to be given something that will serve as an answer, to have to think deeply to find your own, knowing there's more to be said, but what?

Because the penny hadn't dropped and it didn't all make sense – the story of my life and who I am – it came as a surprise when after many years, I realised it was time to end. I don't think I thought of this all by myself – my analyst had dropped hints – but I did suddenly have a clear feeling that it could end and perhaps that it should. Even though I'm not 'fixed' in the way I expected to be.

DOI: 10.4324/9781032637723-37

This is not so long ago and I still think of the analysis and my analyst all the time – through all sorts of moods and thoughts – sadness, regret, anger, gratitude – 'What did she mean by...?', 'I wish I had said/asked.....', 'Why didn't she?...If only she had...if only I had....' I have no doubt I am still in analysis even though we no longer meet. I don't know how long that will go on for or whether the penny will drop. What has changed is that I can bear not knowing – either that or I know more than I think.

Hell Is Other People!

Myth interpretation has many methods. According to folklorist and psychoanalytic apologist Alan Dundes, these methods can be subdivided into either literal or symbolic translations:

> Literalists tend to seek factual or historical bases for a given mythological narrative while advocates of the many symbolic approaches prefer to regard the narrative as a code requiring some mode of decipherment. It is important to realize that the literal and symbolic exegeses of myths are not necessarily mutually exclusive.

In other words, the contradictions that emerge between interpretive approaches do not necessarily undermine their import. For most of my life prior to analysis, contradiction meant death, and my own dreams and aspirations, which operated in mutual exclusion to each other, were the last things I desired to interpret.

At 25, I slipped and stumbled into analysis unknowingly. A failed encounter with what I thought was love left me questioning my own sanity—had I made everything up in my mind? At the time, I was training to become a therapist myself and harbored mild ideological disdain for Freud that I'd gleaned from the texts of Jean-Paul Sartre while studying abroad in Paris. The refrain, "L'enfer c'est les autres [Hell is other people]" resonated so deeply that I had it tattooed on my body as an indelible reminder. Before entering the consulting room for the first time, I had indeed descended into a kind of hell, but with a desperate longing to speak with an other—an authority with whom I might discuss the possibility of redemption.

To my great surprise, the other I found across from me rarely spoke back. Instead, he beckoned me with an enigmatic drift from social propriety—a discourse without words. "If I have something important to say, I'll say it," he told me flatly when I questioned his reticence. Oddly, it was my analyst's relative muteness to which I seemed to owe my relatively quick relief.

Several years passed and my "presenting problem" became an echo. Happily in a new romantic relationship, I felt whole again. I shook my analyst's hand with a smile and bid him farewell only to find myself in the waiting room again four months later after watching my father die. However, this time was different.

DOI: 10.4324/9781032637723-38

Through the hole that my father's death left in my heart, something far more pernicious emerged. Though my first stint in analysis had redeemed me from Hell, new demons appeared, apparently having followed me back to Earth. I became aware of a vast and terrifying lore concerning an epic war between light and darkness, and my conscience demanded that I become the silent hero, never to mention a word about my quest to anyone.

Thus, I began a long period of intransigently mimicking the once supportive muteness of the other across from me in the consulting room. One day, when my analyst recognized that things were teetering precariously on edge, he broke his own silence violently and admonished me as my football coaches had done in my youth. I received this uncharacteristic paroxysm as an indictment—I was failing in my duty as analysand, breaking the sole rule: Speak! The intervention had its intended effect, and I reluctantly began to confess my prophetic visions, opening fresh inquiry into what would eventually reveal itself as the individual myth at the core of my neurosis. It was not until I was forced to interpret this myth that its literal and symbolic forms began to emerge: the apparent discrepancies constituting my biracial heritage, my parents' non-relationship, and my buried ambivalence oozed to the surface, riding and sliding on strings of associations to noxious lead pipes, electromagnetic pollution, and plane crashes.

Light and dark, good and evil, life and death, rich and poor—these were only a few of the seemingly infinite expressions of intractable binaries that haunted my epic, delivering a palpably antagonistic sense of truth. I was Sisyphus grappling with futility—attempting to resolve all contradictions through synthesis. I centered myself as the valiant, yet tortured intermediary—the chosen one who would solve all paradoxes and heal all antinomies. I was slave to the dialectic—I was *Aufhebung* itself. However, reaching sublation meant destroying the others on which I depended, and this was exactly how I viewed having to give the order to take my father off life support.

Over ten years into my analysis, days after I had delivered my first psychoanalytic paper to a room full of others, which bridged the ideas of Donald Winnicott and Jacques Lacan, I found myself unknowingly explaining to my analyst the reasons for anointing myself as the great surgeon, the saving grace, suturing all incompatible sides. My sole desire, which put all other wants and needs on hold, was for oppositional forces to be reconciled, to be harmoniously merged—to bring my black father and white mother together finally in the face of the ills of the world and fix our broken hearts and broken home. I blindly recognized and dutifully repeated this black and white thinking in virtually every area of my life.

I told my analyst that, in researching my paper, it had occurred to me that perhaps the notion of a "good enough father" should accompany Winnicott's "good enough mother"—"good enough" connoting a lack of perfection and ultimate wholeness in the caregiver situation that provides the foundation for a child to find health in maturity and become a unique individual. Undoubtedly sensing that I was on the right track, my analyst once again broke his silence, offering an interpretation of his own: perhaps the conditions in my family had in fact been "good enough" all along.

And in a sudden moment that I can only describe as truly *après-coup*, I sensed being relieved retroactively of my primordial duty to bridge an impossible gap.

The work of Claude Lévi-Strauss attempts to show that the function of myth is to represent and support a fundamental disjunction that could never have been otherwise—myth imbues paradox and antinomy with the ability to foster continuity. Moreover, he contends, myth must be interpreted exhaustively for its true significance to be uncovered. Over time, the interpretations that emerged from within my analysis revealed that I was not failing the hero's role in my individual myth. My myth was merely serving its purpose: holding close the irreconcilable otherness constituting my being and driving my becoming.

A Pair of Converse Trainers

Talking, in previous sessions, about not talking. Not being heard, not feeling listened to, not knowing what to say. All in the context of my analytic training, training people at work, training people in another field. Then, a dream: I see a pair of Converse trainers. I try to interpret, over-intellectualising things as usual. Training... trainers... trainee/trainer.... Am I the trainee or the trainer? Does the dream present an inversion of a trainee-trainer relationship? The inverse, or converse of this, I wonder aloud. Of course, my analyst hears things differently: "Converse." Psychoanalysis has been a very different kind of conversation for me.

DOI: 10.4324/9781032637723-39

My First Wish to Be an Analyst

When I left my native Argentina in 1989, my Buenos Aires's Villa Freud Lacanian friends warned me "Forget the idea of practicing as an analyst in the US. There, psychoanalysis has long been dead. It has been killed decades ago." With this ominous piece of advice, I arrived in the US in the midst of the 1990s so-called "Freud Wars" when calls to "bury Freud" were herd everywhere.

I would introduce myself to new American friends saying "I am an analyst," an affirmation of being that results from the desire produced by an analysis. It is a surprising side effect—someone is in analysis and at some point, as a consequence of this process, desires to become an analyst.

When in 1967 Lacan comes up with the formula that the analyst derives his authorization only from himself/herself, he is highlighting that being an analyst is a not a title granted by an institution: all the institution can do is "provide a guarantee that an analyst has come out of its training." Being an analyst derives from an act of self-authorization located in an area of ambiguity between author (a composer of a work) and authority (having power or control), questioning both the function of an author and of authority. This is a choice that should not be dependent on the big Other (moral duty, law, institutional or social customs, and the like). This radical and simple principle of self-authorization for the training of psychoanalysts involves an ethical decision.

In my own personal history, my first experience of psychoanalysis was as a child, followed by a second analysis as an adolescent, a third one as a young adult, and a last "tranche" or slice in my late twenties until my mid-thirties. I worked with analysts who were Anna-Freudian, Freudian, Kleinian, and Lacanian.

My first memory of a clinical encounter with a psychoanalyst was not truly an analysis but a consultation when I was a five-year-old and needed to have a minor surgery. The school knew of this and promptly sent me to meet with a psychoanalyst at the school's *gabinete psicopedagógico*, a permanent on-site team of a psychoanalyst, a speech therapist, and a school psychologist. The psychoanalyst took me for a course of ten sessions to "prepare" me for the surgery and thus reduce the potential traumatic impact of the surgical procedure. Here, one sees how psychoanalysis had permeated Argentinean culture and institutions. This early and unrequested psychoanalytic intervention was considered standard prophylactic practice.

DOI: 10.4324/9781032637723-40

I spent those sessions making elaborate drawings and speaking about them at length; I recall my deep annoyance facing the recurrent interpretations of the psychoanalyst: I was scared of the surgery and wanted to run away just because there was a girl on a bicycle or a girl riding a car as a recurrent theme. I thought that the lady psychoanalyst was wrong, but I was intrigued by her attempts at finding meaning in my drawings. For me, she was mistaken about the ascribed meanings, but my disagreement meant that there was a hidden meaning ready to be decoded; only she did not capture it.

Six years later, at the age of 11, I started my first psychoanalytic treatment with Dr. Silvia Guarrero, a psychiatrist and psychoanalyst who had an office on a beautiful corner building with a mirador in the roof. In the first session, she explained that in her office I would have a box with art supplies with my name on it. She pointed to shelves with many white boxes opposite the couch on which I was sitting, each with a name tag, and invited me to make a list of what I would want in my box. I asked her for details, and she handed me a pen and paper and told me I could write down what I wanted in the box. "Everything?" I asked. "Everything," she replied. I took her literally and proceeded to write a ten-page list of every possible art supply that exists. When I was done, I proudly handed it to her and was surprised when she told me that she could not get everything on the list; the art supplies had to be restricted to a few items that would fit in the boxes. When I came back to my second session, there was a box with my name waiting, but I noticed that my list (*lista*) of everything had been almost ignored, reduced to a box of markers, some paper, coloured pencils, scissors, and coloured glue. I was not quite ready (*lista*) for the disappointment with which the two-year treatment started. However, it helped me navigate the transition from childhood to adolescence. Now looking back at the signifier that guided the early stages of that first psychoanalytic treatment, I realize that *lista* which means "list," as well as "clever" and "ready" in the feminine form, recurred in *analista*, the Spanish spelling for "analyst."

I had naively believed that I could make a list of my wishes and was confronted with a material limitation that looked like a first prohibition. This may have something to do with the fact that I started writing very early, continuing the metonymic investigation of desired objects, like with my first job as journalist when I was 21 and studying psychoanalysis and psychology. When I was composing imaginary interviews, I could invent what I wanted; the only limit was the credibility gap. As Shakespeare makes Hamlet say, the readiness is all, but my readiness was a readiness to write and the readiness to explore the unconscious.

I became *lista* ("ready") to authorize myself as an analyst, challenging limits because I became *analista* in a context where psychoanalysis was not supposed to happen and I was not expected, supposed or permitted to be acting as a psychoanalyst. I had carefully rephrased and in some places erased the very word "psychoanalysis" from my resume to secure getting hired as a "staff psychologist" in my first job in a barrio clinic in the late 1980s.

But it was in that context, in an office that did not have an analytic couch but had enough space to recreate a quasi-Freudian stage that I found myself positioned as an analyst, sustaining the hypothesis of the unconscious, asking my patients to freely associate and talk about their dreams. In my ample consulting room in the Centro de Servicios para Hispanos, in a decrepit building that had been a funeral home in better times, I became *analista* maybe because, as Lacan suggests, I was in the position of the "dummy"—I was playing dead. My office, with incongruously elaborate flower carvings in the wall's wood panelling and its tired, lumpy brownish-orange carpet had been the room where coffins would be displayed for visitation. I would sit with the enormous beaten-up steel Tanker desk behind me, while my "clients," as we were asked to call the people we served, using a term that offered them illusory empowerment as economic agents, because healthcare is a business like any other, were provided with battered chairs. I invited my patients to become analysands, asking them to sit looking at the window, facing away from my gaze so as to avoid the face-to-face model of interpersonal relationships. To say that the barrio was tough is an understatement; on a daily basis, one of my patients would report a crime-related death. There was once a drive-by shooting in the middle of the day, just under my office windows. From time to time, while watering the plants in the office, I thought of the rows of wooden coffins that had been laid in that room for viewing.

In that context, I would tell my patients to say whatever comes to mind, giving myself the freedom to take distance from the prevalent mandates of the therapeutic model of orthopaedics of the mind. Not knowing anything about family therapy or cognitive therapy and having no interest in engaging in a pedagogical modality of treatment, I discovered myself by default working as an analyst. I was practicing in an environment hostile to conceiving that psychoanalytic work with poor and disenfranchised minority people in a ghetto setting was not possible. I made a choice that granted me freedom and helped me survive in a challenging setting. My position as an analyst was linked to the authority provided by my awareness that the poor are poor but can afford an unconscious.

To authorize oneself is a forced choice, not dependent on the big Other, just on some others. Lacan also talks about choice when he proposes that when confronted with sexual difference or sexuation, one needs to take sides. There is a "male side" that is linked to phallic enjoyment and a "female side" whose form of enjoyment is not fully subjected to the phallus. These two positions are not determined by biology but by the logic of unconscious investments, to the point that, for instance, a cis male can nevertheless inscribe himself on the female side. Freed from the shackles of anatomy, the assumption of a gendered positioning has to do with self-authorization in speech. Here, the idea is that the authorization of a subject as a sexual being (man, woman or anything else) originates in oneself; that is, in matters of sexual difference, one proceeds from one's own authorization. Sexual positioning like self-authorization for the analyst is placed in this area of ambiguity between author and authority. The phrase is a variant of Lacan's aphorism: "the analyst authorizes himself/herself." To authorize oneself as a man, woman or something else altogether involves an ethical decision, as also happens when pondering the position an analyst should adopt. Here psychoanalytic ethics meets a new ethics of sexual difference.

I became *analista*—I authorized myself as a psychoanalyst—and went across an impossible crossroads in a place where psychoanalysis was not expected to happen. But isn't psychoanalysis, as Freud notes, like governing and educating, an impossible profession? Being a Lacanian is not being any kind of Freudian but a political Freudian, that is, a critical Freudian and at times I am a critical Lacanian as well, an analyst who intervenes in the field to redefine it and reinvent it—a perfect wish list.

An Excerpt from a Didactic Analysis
Death in Other Words

I remember telling my analyst about visiting an ossuary whilst on holiday abroad. In that session, I was speaking about how fascinating I found the display of bones and mummified monks, and I went on to explain how, in my 20s, I would always seek out cemeteries in foreign countries. I seemed to have developed an interest in how different cultures bury their dead and how cemeteries are in different countries. My analyst was interested in my words 'mummified monks', and as I spoke more about it, I found myself talking about my father, who had died when I was 20. The sessions that followed revolved around how my father had died, abroad and far away, on the other side of the world. He had been buried before I found out he had died, and I had never been able to visit his grave.

My relationship with my father had been complicated. However, I had always been puzzled by how little I had felt about his death at the time, and in the years following his death, I would often think that I had seen him in the streets, which would fill me with dread. Speaking about the ossuary and cemeteries and their emerging relation to my father's death took me by surprise. I started having dreams, and two of particular significance stand out. I dreamt I was on an island (my father died on an island), and on the top of this island, there was a castle ruin. Inside the castle was a mummy, embellished with jewellery, which I associated to him. In another dream, I found a rotting arm in the ocean, which I associated to my father who I thought had caused me 'h-arm', both in life and in death. Through this process in analysis, I came to realise I hadn't accepted my fathers' death, and I was terrified both of accepting he was dead but at the same time of the thought he might still be alive. That session which started out a simple retelling of a holiday, and a visit to an ossuary changed a lot for me. The word 'mummy' turned out not to be only related to my father: it seemed to evoke other significant relationships and meanings for me, and my analyst's particular interest in those words 'mummified monks' seemed to have started my own process of interpreting death and my relationship with it.

DOI: 10.4324/9781032637723-41

Image of a Telephone

During Lacan's Seminar 1971–72 '... *ou Pire*' ('... or Worse'), he recounts that he had recently been given a pen by someone, an admirer, who might be in the audience '.., I made use of this pen straightaway to do some writing, and this is where my reflections began. It's when I am writing that I find something.'

When we went into lockdown, I continued my analysis by phone. I liked the idea of a disembodied voice and a disconnected connection between two scenes. For me analysis was all about the voice, the words and the act of speaking. Speaking by phone meant that there were no distractions, only the words in their abstracted form along with their musicality and performativity.

My life as a musician had suddenly come to a halt after over 30 years of constantly being on the move, recording and performing. Everything had seemed to have come to a standstill, apart from my analysis and dreams. I remember in particular a sequence of dreams around the theme of railway stations, mostly in black and white film noir style. In the final dream, the station was Brussels, one that I had travelled through numerous times with my quartet on European tours, *Brussels Midi* being the centre of a network spreading out to many cities in Europe. The telephone came to take centre stage in this final dream of the sequence.

In my free associations around the dream, I was in the middle of speaking about an aspect of it when suddenly I heard the dialling tone. Rather shocked at first I then smiled, how could my analyst have the cheek to hang up on me! But then there followed a sense of trust I had in him and that I felt he had in me. After all, surely he would not have done something so dramatic if this was not the case.

In my thoughts about the dream, it was my analyst who had entered into the scene but now the telephone handset was hanging by its cotton wound wire and this was all that was left of my analyst. He had left the scene, like a detective slipping into the shadows, leaving me to find my own way out of this large space busy with movement across invisible diagonal lines directing the commuters in their grey uniform suits.

Why had my analyst left the scene? Why had I been deserted? What exactly was the word that my analyst cut me off on? Was this the end of my analysis? In the context of analysis, these weren't just questions about how a phone call ended but

DOI: 10.4324/9781032637723-42

existential questions about my position in the world and my relationship to other people, not just my relationship to my analyst and psychoanalysis.

The image of a telephone connected me to my past. I am 13 years of age and I'm at boarding school, in the middle of Dorset. It is winter and the memory image is again monochrome. In the atrium of the large Victorian mansion is a glass wooden framed telephone box with coin-operated phone. This was the scene of many phone calls I had made to my family home, miles away in sunny Surrey. Through my tears I would hear the kettle boiling and my two sisters happy and laughing in the echoey kitchen. Mum, who would often answer the phone, never knew what to say because I would be crying, wanting to come home, and this wasn't an option. She had taken on a new job in order to pay for my school fees, and there were no local schools which would offer such a substantial music scholarship. 'Just give it one more term …' mum would repeat each successive term… 'just give it one more term', until I gave up the struggle and resigned myself. What helped me through the psychodrama of the early days of boarding school was my music. Music was a world that I could escape into and re-find the feeling of love and enjoyment that I had lost.

Writing about the dream today, I can see how the intervention, the cut in the dream work, provoked a change in the memory of boarding school and reminded me of the solace that music gave me as it linked me to the sounds of my family home. I realised that the trajectory of my career was born out of a loss, a loss of maternal enjoyment. This cut in the session opened up a new desire for knowledge and the separation of interrelated themes to create the possibility of a different knot of consistency.

This could sound like a straightforward process, but the truth is that it was the result of many returns to the related scenes to reform or rewrite those memories. The phone was a nodal point in a network of signifiers that tied in directly with my career as a musician. The process of the analysis amounted to patiently cutting away at the ties, session after session, each return to the related scenes subtracted and emptied out meaning, turning what I saw as my truth into a desire for knowledge. The process was retro-affective: in other words, each return modulated my feelings and underlying structures.

Perhaps the abrupt ending of the phone call was one of many short endings that would eventually lead to the final end of my analysis. This is how it might happen … the dialling tone … the walking out of the door for the last time …. It would simply end … but what would be put in motion by the analysis would continue, the cut and the creation of an opening and a desire for more knowledge.

A Story

Reflecting on how change has come about in analysis brings up various thoughts and experiences from the work. I had intuited that something might change by undertaking a work of therapy or analysis, and recall writing to my prospective analyst that something in life was 'holding me back'. Beginning the work, whatever shape it would eventually take, came with the belief that this something would shift, that there would be a movement of sorts which would allow for change to take place.

In our first session, rather terrified, and sat across from somebody I did not know, I spoke about my life in terms of a rather broad trajectory: there were a set of key people involved, a beginning and a middle part, then followed by the suffering and set of problems I found myself with at that time. Some of these difficulties seemed continuous, and others specific to that present moment.

The response met with was that I had been presenting a story. A very simple observation, at least so in hindsight, but it was a very powerful thing to hear. Perhaps the reason it was so powerful was because I was well aware that my involvement in such narratives was a big part of why I found myself there at all. I had for some time found myself caught up in versions of stories that did not speak to my experience, to the way I saw things, and yet they were defining me, somehow.

To be a bit more specific, there was a version of events about who I was in relation to my immediate family and who everyone else was within that archipelago. A not insignificant aspect of this was the sexed nature of the problematic, and with a father who had passed away some years before, something I struggled with was the narrative that had been established about who he had been, and who myself and the others had been and continued to be in relation to him.

So, there was a story about what had happened in my past and ideas about how it all affected me, coupled with the recognition that it involved my relating to other people. This, in the context of a talking therapy, presented a preliminary or potential solution to these problems: to put them into dialogue.

During the first few months of analysis, whilst beginning to articulate what was troubling me, I had the idea that my grievances might be put to those with whom I struggled the most, where my problems were currently being played out in a messy, difficult way. The dialogue here would be had with other people. It may have been

DOI: 10.4324/9781032637723-43

inevitable for me at some point to have brought about such confrontations, along with the assumption that some things needed to be said and that it would bring about a change not only in the way I felt, but that it could have a positive impact on those relationships. Unsurprisingly to my analyst, however, my attempt to do so did not help in the way I expected it to.

Nonetheless, there was a lesson to be learned there, which I came to think of as a question about what might change internally for me, without the necessity of a demonstrable change in a set of relations to others; that there would always be a discrepancy between my expectations and my immediate reality, and perhaps that it was even something to be cherished. Or to go further, that the continuous return, through interpretation or intervention, to the points at which perceived or stated expectations of my own and others met, or faltered, or caused anguish, were what sustained and helped me 'move through' the work over the years.

That is not to say that some concrete steps shouldn't ever be taken, or that material changes, or trying to say what may have previously been unthinkable to a significant other, in one's life, cannot be useful. There was something very tangible about the place and the effects certain others have had in mine, and would go as far as to say that some measures I've taken to deal with the problem of proximity, either by separating or conversely by seeking closeness, may have saved me on occasion.

The point I would choose to focus on here, however, is that there was something to be reckoned with in terms of a 'hard-wiring', one which can be an external circumstance involving someone else with their own set of symptoms, such as a person it is difficult to keep from encroaching on different aspects of, for example, my life, but also to see that the more the question of other people's aspirations and plans are spoken about, the more you end up speaking of your own, and that taking a form of ownership of this view is a long way from speaking about narratives imposed upon you from without.

The only analytic intervention I have mentioned in this short piece is that it was pointed out I had been speaking about, and through, a story. This was a way for me to situate my suffering in a new way and would, over time, be complicated and re-elaborated. I'm of the view that my own and indeed the stories of the people I work with clinically are evolving ones, with an importance given to outlining a frame to delineate where what is being said has precedent, where words are charged or ambiguous, and how they try to capture what cannot be included in the story.

Eat What You Want, Drink What You Want

For years in my analysis, I had spoken of the difficult relationship I had with my father. He was an alcoholic and drinking ultimately killed him. He acted as if drinking was his right, and I had found this liberalism disingenuous and uncaring, whilst also feeling an urgent sense of responsibility to limit it. My inability to do so was a source of great pain after his death. He had died only a few months after my first analysis had begun, and so initially there was an immediacy to the topic. I noted that not long after his death, he was rarely present in my dreams, though when so, he was a sympathetic, undead figure, lost and unknowing of his own demise. Later, he began to appear more frequently, no longer undead or so uncertain of himself.

In time, I drifted further from the scene of my father's death and my narrative crystallised. He was complicated, though a good man, unable to manage his burdens but always trying his best. There was a nobility to him perhaps, unsuited to deal with the hand he'd been dealt, finding the changing world of work and the break-up of his marriage difficult. I was angry with his behaviour, though also empathised and even identified with him. He was troubled, yet I loved and missed him. Time went by with little new said about him, and it became a challenge to shift beyond the narrative I had pieced together.

At a certain point in my analysis, I began to notice feeling more reactive in my day-to-day encounters with friends and family. I was taking positions which felt out of character, and I was noticeably sensitive and critical, in a way which to me felt unusual and out of my control. This came to a head in a series of encounters which had me responding critically in discussions around eating, drinking and casual drug use. My own criticisms sounded oddly conservative, and I felt a jarring separation between my supposed beliefs and what I was saying.

I took this upset into my analysis and my analyst enquired as to the details. I told them about the feeling of unease I'd experienced, specifically around the topic of 'casual' consumption. 'This stuff matters', I argued, 'at a certain stage you can't just eat what you want and drink what you want without it having consequences for others!' My analyst offered back the sentence 'eat what you want, drink what you want', stopping my complaint in its tracks.

The intervention removed the prohibiting 'can't', which had the effect of loosening the more critical and accusatory imperatives of my complaint. Importantly,

DOI: 10.4324/9781032637723-44

I felt it focussed attention on the 'want' of my speech. It also evoked on the years of scrutiny regarding my own troubling bodily excesses and limitations, and the often obsessive and debilitating micro-management of dietary habits and inhibitions. It refocused my criticism, hollowing out a space to recognise the place from where I criticised. My righteous indignation around casual consumption now felt rhetorical and the context of my anger felt false. The stories I had told of my father and our relationship, useful in their own ways, hadn't touched on the impossibilities of it. My anger and self-imposed restrictions, physical and psychical, now felt like positions in relation to a careless, callous liberalism.

There was little casual about my own tightly cautious approach to consumption. For me, 'eat what you want, drink what you want' addressed an impossibility, and in response the tapestry of personal boundaries and limitations I imposed. The intervention of my analyst had not rationally countered my complaint of course, rather the specificity and context of the words in that moment had helped blur my target, allowing room for my aggression to shift from rhetoric to dialectic. This separation, carved out between my own body and my father's, allowed space for a dialogue to occur between him and I. Speaking to the limits I imposed on myself could now also be an engagement with his lack of limits. The particular texture of our relationship, its singular points of pressure, could be treated as a vocabulary, and the aggressive restrictions directed towards myself and others treated as an elaboration of my relation to him.

As in my dreams of my father, sympathy could perhaps soften, moving towards greater engagement with his agency and my own, working responsively with one another. The analysis of my aggressive inhibitions could now be considered research, a want to find some form of answer to punishing and painful questions. What had driven my father to act as he did, and what had driven me to participate?

A Sewing Machine
and an Umbrella

Thanks to this invitation to write, I went back to the memories of my decade-long, twice-weekly Lacanian analysis. Having discovered psychoanalysis in my philosophy class during my last year of secondary school, I had already held it in high regard. Someone could help me decipher what was at stake, beyond all reasoning and conventions! When, years later, I decided to actually start an analysis, my encounter with my analyst was decisive and oriented my whole life.

If I were to choose a word to describe my first years of analysis, it would be a "whirlwind": of ideas, creativity, questions and actions. It meant opening up to the realm of desire and libido…I felt passion at every level of my life!

Contrary to the stereotype of the silent psychoanalyst, my analyst was fairly vocal – not all the time of course, he could stay very quiet, but when he intervened in different ways (by asking questions, repeating my words, interpreting or explaining his point), his words resonated strongly, even when I did not understand them immediately. Often it would only be while running down the stairs or walking down the street that, in a flash, his words would suddenly make sense.

Coming to my sessions was most of the time a pleasure, even a thrill. I came expecting something to happen and most often it did, and I was baffled by the outcome. My analyst would challenge my assumptions, disrupting my certainties. In talking about what I was going through, more than once I described as a consequence what was actually the cause, the core of my thoughts and actions. It was as if I was given another lens to look differently at my motivations, what was driving me or, let's not be afraid of the word, my desire.

Those first years of analysis were an intense time of experimentation, creativity, as well as some big life decisions. They were fuelled by intense dreams, which I would bring into my sessions. Dreams were a crucial part of this work, and they really revealed to me what the unconscious was: something that couldn't be tamed and instead was driving me. I scrutinised them with my analyst, who picked on the details, on the way I would say things. This often amazed me – a word or even a simple sound could have a meaning, one that I hadn't been aware of prior to deciphering the somehow playful logic of the dream.

The work was not easy and was often destabilising, as if a wall of convictions was slowly but surely being demolished, brick by brick. I think that I was only able

DOI: 10.4324/9781032637723-45

to bear it because my analyst handled things with such warmth and humour…we laughed a lot!

Let me give you a fun example of a session revolving around a dream and its deciphering. Coming to the session that day, I thought the dream was quite silly, but I couldn't find anything else to talk about.

A doctoral student in literature, I was soon to give my first seminar to university students. I was extremely nervous by the prospect, worrying I wouldn't do well enough.

The dream was that I was in the classroom, and suddenly the students turned into shoes and parakeets. At the end of the hour, I stroke the shoes and the parakeets – the latter seemed especially happy, the feathers on their heads pointing up and their eyes spinning.

To give you a bit of context, as a child I had once had a parakeet, which very much enjoyed being stroked under its beak and on its head.

My analyst enquired first about the shoes: what kind of shoes were they? The shoes in my dream were made of leather, but it was faux crocodile leather. He instantly made a joke, asking if La Fontaine had in fact written a fable called "The Parakeet and the Crocodile!" He carried on:

> Don't you think that this dream sounds a bit like Alice in Wonderland – but here it is a menagerie?! It also makes one think of the "Chance encounter on a dissecting table of a sewing machine and an umbrella!"

> (a famous line from de Lautréamont's The Songs of Maldoror)

As an association, I said I'd been looking for a pair of shoes the previous weekend. I had found a pair I really liked, but the salesperson couldn't find the left shoe and asked me to come back on Monday, which was the day of the dream. I added that the model was called "Blossoming" – "A pretty name", my analyst reacted. I then suddenly remembered that in my dream, the faux croc leather shoes had a hole at the toe. "This is normal", my analyst asserted, "that's the mouth! Every word you say is weighed, calibrated, hence the shoe is a *semblant* of the crocodile. The aim is that the crocodile doesn't eat you, and that the parakeet repeats!"

I added that I also wanted the students to be happy, because in my dream the parakeets seemed to enjoy being stroked, with their feathers pointing up and eyes rolled back, to which he replied, "The way you act, they will undoubtedly be happy!"

I left laughing, relieved somehow by the prospect of this first class I would be teaching the following day and thinking that indeed, no dream is foolish.

The Hidden Letter

Once upon a time, it feels like ages now, I was lying on the couch, lamenting my impossibility to choose between two men. I know, it sounds very obnoxious. It's not as if they were sitting in a reception room waiting for their turn. Anyhow, I had started dating an architect and my great love, who had left me, seemed to want to get back with me. Whom should I choose? The man who had broken my heart or the architect who might bring some order into my life? There must be a reason why Freemasons call God the "the great architect of the universe," I said to my analyst and continued: "The first is envious and melancholic, the second expansive and cheerful, is a good lover and reads Marx in bed next to me, wearing a Stanford sweater." My psychoanalyst sat quietly as usual, but this time his silence was particularly straining. "Whom shall I choose? Please say something!" But he remained silent, like an absent God. I sensed my anger lingering beneath the surface and left the session as if I had a rocket in my ass. My psychoanalyst followed me through the waiting room and remained in the doorway of the building watching me disappear, like in a movie, as if it was him I was about to leave. It was Friday and I was going away with my best friend and her boyfriend to visit another couple who lived happily in a castle in the countryside, on the beautiful coast of Normandy. I was literally going to be the fifth wheel, but who says no to a few days by the sea?

"I have chosen!" were my first words back on the couch. I told my analyst how I had found myself sitting alone, in a café, while my friends were visiting a 1,200-year-old oak tree, when suddenly I had seen several older men dressed in uniforms appearing on the terrace of the cafe, greeting each other, and toasting in schnapps glasses. The scene felt a little surreal. I asked an elderly gentleman with a beret, moustache, and rosy cheeks who was sitting close to me what they were doing here. "It's the D-Day Festival, don't you know your history Mademoiselle?" A few minutes later, I was sitting like a small child, absorbed in his stories. He was only seven years old back then, but he remembers it like yesterday, the day when two German officers on the run had rushed into their house at night, in search of a bed and some food. Before they disappeared the next day, the young boy managed to see one soldier's scarf, which had a text embroidered in both French and German: "If I advance, follow me, if I retreat, kill me." This phrase struck me like lightening. When my friends returned from their excursion, I asked them to help

DOI: 10.4324/9781032637723-46

me choose between the two men, adding the fateful sentence. They laughed and thought that I should first of all decide what I wanted in life and then figure out which one of the two men was most likely to accept my desires. I listed all my requests and concluded that the architect was most likely to accept them. I decided to write him a letter containing all my desires in the form of a contract, like a devil's pact, which I did, back in the car, on a piece of paper. I took it out of my pocket now and started reading it aloud to my analyst. He said nothing. I felt a little bit ashamed, claiming it was not a grocery list but a true act of desire. When I left the room, I said to him: "You know, the funny thing is that it is the other man I want and not the architect, but as the German officer suggested: "If I advance, follow me, if I retreat, kill me." Another friend laughed ironically at me saying "You let a dead German Nazi soldier decide for you, good for you!""

On Wednesday afternoon, it was time for the customary psychoanalytical seminar I attended once a week, which was run by my analyst. This time we were studying an article dealing with the difference between "passage à l'acte" and "acting out." When the presenter of the text touched on the difference between the two actions, in the first case the ultimate interlocutor is death, and in the second, the act is mostly addressed to the psychoanalyst, and has to be recognised and interpreted; otherwise, it would repeat itself *ad infinitum*. I was struck with severe dizziness. Was the letter's actual addressee my own analyst? In a way yes, I had written a love letter to him, by hand some months earlier, that I carried around for a while before losing it. He was forbidden after all. An hour later I was lying on his couch again and heard myself asking him: "Do you think my letter was actually addressed to you?" My analyst suddenly answered: "Yes!". I couldn't believe my ears. I had been secretly in love with him for almost a year, trying to interpret every little ambiguous gesture of his part, and now, I was exposed, like a thief caught with my pants down. "A letter always reaches its destination," replied my psychoanalyst laconically from his chair with a clear wink of course to Edgar Allan Poe's "The Purloined Letter," famously analysed by Lacan.

My analysis took a whole new turn after this point. The revelation of my hidden letter both freed me from my inhibition, which until then had forced me to beat about the bush, instead of speaking about it, and put my transference love in motion, creating all kinds of unexpected turning points; I've not entirely understood yet, but what I can clearly say now is that my analysis eventually became a space where I began to seriously examine the meaning of impossible love in my life. It confronted me with a much bigger choice: did I want to remain a passive, loved object, or like Alcibiades who, thanks to Socrates' resistance, became an active loving subject unafraid to act upon my desires? I also realised that authentic relations need no contracts, but the careful day-by-day construction opened up to the unexpected. I now dare to loose myself and advance in all directions, both the future and the past, helping my own patients to do the same. Had I not met that older man and heard his story, talked to my friends about it, written and read the letter on the couch, attended the seminar some days later and finally received an answer from my analyst, I might still be torn between the two men, and like Buridan's obsessional ass, which, incapable of choosing between two options, starves to death. It is the act that frees us, the choice that saves us when it disrupts the jouissance of indecision, even if it sometimes has to take the detour of a misdirected letter.

Scrambled Eggs

Not long into the first session of my abortive first consultation with a psychoanalyst, I unexpectedly found myself talking about a panic attack I'd had some years previously when, unbeknownst to me, my life was rapidly unravelling.

The analyst asked me to describe what happened. I'd cooked scrambled eggs for some university friends, I told him, and we were watching a film, when the disturbing conviction had imposed itself on me that I was about to die.

"What was the film?"

Oh, I wavered, it was called "The Machinist". But that wasn't what I wanted to talk about.

"What's it about?"

It was about unconscious guilt. But I hastily added that I didn't think that was relevant to the panic attack which, I insisted, must have been "entirely chemical" (I'd taken some dodgy pills at a club a few nights previously). I told him that although it was true that I hadn't gone back to the film since, it stood to reason that I'd avoid anything whatsoever that had some connection to that night.

"Did you avoid scrambled eggs?"

I felt a pang of anxiety, managed a feeble "N... no", and was momentarily lost for words. He stood up abruptly and ushered me out.

DOI: 10.4324/9781032637723-47

The Eye of the Storm

The most useful interpretation I have received in an analysis was during my first psychoanalytic treatment (I have undergone three analyses), which occurred when I was in graduate school studying for a Doctorate in Clinical Psychology. As I relayed more and maore of my history to the analyst, I reached the point where it was time to discuss the most traumatic period of my life. It was 1992, and I had just been picked up from Lollapalooza by my high school boyfriend's father, who informed us during the car ride home that there was a hurricane coming. Growing up in Miami, there was always a storm brewing. But this one was different. Hurricane Andrew was a category five and was the worst storm to ever hit the United States until Hurricane Katrina in 2005. It is still the worst storm to ever hit Florida.

My boyfriend's family invited me to stay at their house, but my parents understandably wanted me to be with them, so they picked me up. After my father helped some friends board up their homes, we headed down south to weather the storm in the winter home of friends of the family. My parents assumed we would be better off in a newer construction, rather than in our home, which was built in 1913, constantly under construction, and already had a leaky roof. Unfortunately, heading further south landed us directly in the path of the hurricane, and we ended up in the eye of the storm.

Following the aftermath of Hurricane Andrew, my parents got divorced. When kicking my father out of the house didn't solve all of her problems, my mother asked me to leave, too. I was 15 years old, soon to be 16.

"The same age as your mother when she was sent away."

This interpretation struck me to my core. When my mother was 16, she was married to her father's military buddy and sent off to Germany to live where he was stationed. She never saw her mother again, as her mother died in childbirth with a younger sibling. The baby died, too.

Having such a hugely traumatic event as Hurricane Andrew occur, an event that literally destroyed our home, just when I reached the age my mother was when she was torn away from her family, never to be able to return home again, sent my mother into a downward spiral from which she's never fully recovered. It tore our family apart, and 30 years later, we're still sifting through the rubble.

DOI: 10.4324/9781032637723-48

Understanding that we can have such intense reactions, and have material resurface when our children reach the age we were when we experienced such trauma, has become essential to my practice. I often encourage analysands to be mindful of this if they have children.

As severe natural disasters become more and more commonplace due to climate emergency, I have also begun to understand Hurricane Andrew as a prelude to the many storms to come. I become frustrated, infuriated even, when the media presents the death toll and dollar cost of such disasters, failing to take into consideration the many lives that have been affected, the destinies that have been intractably rerouted, the broken homes that follow, and the trauma that affects people for the rest of their lives. The toll is much greater than anyone seems to care to admit. Hopefully psychoanalysis can be a place where these stories are told, connections are made, and understanding may come into being.

Swift and Fragmentary Notes on Interpretation

Only what matters does matter

Sometimes spelled out, determined or grave, interpretation can also be light, agile, allusive and perplexing. In one way or another, it is a matter of eliciting what matters, what is at stake in whatever painful inertia an analysand suffers. Deft by chance, ponderous by mistake, and nimble if possible.

1

There are often interventions which emphasise the logic of a statement and its possible transformations, such as affirmation – negation, active – passive tenses, substitutions of (im)personal pronouns, singular – plural, and general – singular.

- 'My mother would have never said that!'
- 'Who would?' Or – 'And thought that?' Or – 'Not once!'

Grammar and logic are great movable tongues, switching points. They can suddenly make an unexpected viewpoint appear. They may also help to elicit a core which is rather impervious to these syntactic permutations, a core of intransigent (and strange) satisfaction.

2

- '(...) farther'.
- 'What has your father to do with this?'
- 'My father? I wasn't talking about my father.... Ah! No, I said farther, further...'.

'But now that you said that..., actually,...'
So even mishearing can lead to an unexpected opening!

DOI: 10.4324/9781032637723-49

3

For the nth time he was re-telling the same particular story…

- 'Have you not told me this before?' the analyst asked kindly, with a pinch of irony.

The analysand laughed, and the analyst never heard that story again – at least never told in the same way.

Interpretation can be allusive, humorous, may sometimes elicit what is hidden in repetition but also what repetition enjoys.

4

- 'Now I don't know what to say…'
- 'I take your word for it.'

But perhaps it would have been simpler to end the session on that. It is not easy to elicit the passage between words and deed.

5

For a while he was concerned …'blablabla… by…I'm thinking… about writing… and more blablabla about it…'
A fter a while – a number of sessions, the analyst, with a tone of logical bonhomie,

- 'You want to write? Well…, write!'

What matters is not always to understand why this, and why that but to pass through the quest of meaning, to act. To *de-cide* (from de, 'off', + *caedere*, 'cut', bring to a settlement – even a temporary one).

Interpretation does not always problematise, enlighten or reframe, which, as useful as it is, opens the path to infinity and beyond. At its most acute, interpretation, logically or otherwise, prompts decision.

6

A dream:

- '(…) and a black postman gave me something. I don't remember what, a parcel probably or a letter. But I don't understand why a black postman…?'
- 'Blackmail?'

That produced some relevant associations.

The manifest narrative is a story not to be explained but to be heard. Understanding is not the crux of the matter but the stake is.

7

A psychoanalyst listens and considers that anything said counts but the meaning of what is said is not what is most important to determine but rather the path that elicits the cul-de-sac of meaning is.

What would a conclusive (even not final) interpretation be?

Something that renders something problematic less problematic, not problematic any more.

- ' am fed up to have to be what other people want me to be!'
- [silence]
- 'You don't believe me?'
- 'Sure.'
- 'You think I want to be what people want me to be?'
- [silence]
- '..., well, you may be right.'

Silence gives rise to assumptions, and may make them, and what is at stake in them, manifest.

Interpretation unsettles what is entrenched, gives some equilibrium to what cannot find sufficient stabilisation and, from a tweak to a transformation, contributes to a new economy of enjoyment (jouissance). In brief, interpretation participates in the general endeavour of psychoanalytic practice. Take any situation as an occasion and, beyond this, elicit a point of passage through ... through something vain.

Scansion

Sex

I entered analysis as a young and beautiful 21-year-old, a seductive hysteric, passionate about psychoanalysis. I was aware of my sexual charm but troubled by my voraciousness. I developed an eating disorder that lasted for almost two years. I would binge and purge and find relief in filling myself up to then empty myself by force. I suffered shame and guilt but could not find a way to stop this despised repetition.

My parents somehow knew of my sexual impetus, because those things are unconsciously communicated, and so they wanted to control me. A Catholic conservative mother, and a much more flexible father who obeyed his woman for love, I had the fate of living with them until marriage, preferably in a virgin state.

I found a young analyst, arriving from the crib of psychoanalysis with a brand new PhD. My imaginary fascination back then with anything foreign, in addition to the analyst's seductive charm, was a catalyst for the development of a substantial erotomania that fortunately undid the initial symptom in only a few months. A simple Lacanian cut of the session at the 5-minute mark increased agitated my fury. My ego ideal, always identified with the good girl, turned into a furious bitch, validating the sayings of my mother "a wolf in a sheep's clothing." I refused to leave the office, while the analyst waited patiently at the door. I threw my sunglasses at him and deliberately missed the target, then left the office dramatically. That cut had effects and I started thriving in my studies, building friendships and devouring whatever I could find on psychoanalysis, art, literature or film. Finally, I had sexual experiences beyond the idiotic boyfriend that came together with the symptom. Those were three years of marvellous growth, I graduated with honours, travelled, and found a job in an organization that exposed me to a rich clinical practice. I supervised clinical cases with my analyst and one other supervisor, and I started to learn how to guide my listening.

Love

I found love, dazzling, overwhelming, beautiful. After a few months, I got married to the love of my life and left the analysis. After a couple of years, however,

DOI: 10.4324/9781032637723-50

I came back to analysis, having transformed myself into a subdued wife, covering my body, hiding my radiance for fear of increasing my always relentless desire to feel desired. I worked through some insights about femininity, which opened my sexual drive in my marriage. I pursued more studies and took seriously my desire to become an analyst. The erotomania, or sexual transference, had decreased, but the attraction continued albeit less wildly.

I convinced the analyst that I had finished my analysis. I was a parrot repeating theory. I embellished my plot with the true effects of my analysis. But the erotomania was intact and what was the hurry anyhow? To my surprise, the analyst proposed that we choose a day as a last session. Bad idea. An end of analysis is not a motion of the analyst. The analyst can never enunciate such an event. The day arrived and I left the analyst's office feeling proud of my "end of analysis" after about five years in total.

Fantasy

One year after I had left analysis, I was happily pregnant. One more year later, seeking possibilities to work on a project, I visited the ex-analyst and not expecting it, although desiring it, we made out. And then again and again after that. Never beyond the secretive, never outside the office. Bad idea. There was no end of analysis because the erotomania had not been resolved and instead of traversing the fantasy (my parent's sexual elan) I acted it out. I was full, I was triumphant, and I had gotten partially what fantasmatically I desired so compulsively. It was devastating. Life conditions became challenging when I moved to another country with my family. That brief bliss was paid for with a few years of intense suffering. The immigration process unmoored and uprooted me from the solid amorous social bond of my culture and extended family. I would have wanted to engross myself in the imaginary phallic sense of self of those intoxicating brief months. Not possible. Instead, I became a malfunctioning boat lost in a cold sea. Had I ended my analysis, I would have developed a way of dealing with my lack (mistakes, flaws, insecurities) and the need to stand up for myself. It was dark for a while. Because of my sexual desire and the lack of knowing how to deal with it, certain feminine devaluations started to emerge. A negative fantasy, the reverse of the imaginary phallic Woman, started to unfold. Inherited from the vicious feminine patriarchy of my lineage that claimed: "a man sleeps with whomever he wants and remains dignified as ever, a woman instead stays in a pool of dirt," the negative fantasy made me a self-deprecating victim, hurt and angry, lashing out at myself and my loved ones.

Death

I looked for another analyst, but it was not possible to meet remotely, only in person. I would travel to meet him on vacations and had daily sessions, sometimes twice a day, for two weeks at a time. There were probably three series of this accelerated analysis. My beloved father died, the most significant loss, my pillar, my anchor, a force of life. I dealt with it in analysis. Also, I wanted to establish psychoanalysis in my new city and the difficulties appeared overwhelming. "It will take time," the analyst told me convincingly. Something of his listening allowed me to process traumatic situations caused by the imaginary impotence of "being The Woman," which could not sustain me in times of duress. He cut a session to punctuate my fantasy of not paying the price. There is indeed an exorbitant subjective payment when jouissance is not relinquished by the analyst in the transference, past or present. Then there is no analytic act but exploitation. I had learned such a price in the flesh; I could articulate it now. Then my new analyst passed away peacefully one night. He had a certain warmth in his way of listening and I was sad, yet not devastated. He left and left me in a much better place. I said goodbye from a distance, thankful and calm.

Hate

A few years later, I asked an esteemed colleague, a friend from the Sigmund-world, to supervise some cases with me. One session he said, "It seems that there are some articulations needed here," and proposed to move from supervision to analysis. I was furious; he had ethically betrayed me. I worked with him for about three years. His style was conducive to generating negative reactions. One time he forced me to pay for sessions when I was on vacation. I hated him. I cried every time I finished a session. The transferential hate opened up my own internalized racism, patriarchy, ageism. I embodied a radical difference. I had to renounce being the One Woman who could do it all, and instead, I hosted my castration with grace and dignity and a joyful statement emerged: "I err, and yet I stand by myself." I listened more freely to my analysands, and a style was emerging with quiet confidence, beyond persecutory dogma or pretentiousness. My mother died of cancer, and I accepted her inherited difficulties while recognizing her warmth and loving care. I indulge in my love for life and my love of dancing. The latter articulates something of the body that escapes the word; it knots something of my fire. I won't burn. I struggle following some choreographies and the superego back then, not losing a chance to inject death into a body, repeated "You do not know how to dance," making me feel self-conscious, insecure, and tense. Even though I know I am not that bad, not at all.

Jouissance

In a psychoanalytic conference, a mature man describes a dream in which he is lying in a bed with his penis connected, through a strange tubular mechanism, to a dog under the bed, who sucks up his semen. That night, sleeping alone in my hotel room, I had a paradigmatic dream that unknotted my symptomatic sexual conundrum. I dreamt that my beloved husband told me, "You do not know how to dance," and I woke up with an orgasm. Disturbed by the transparency, with liberated thought and a quiet joy acquired with the revelation of this blunt truth,

I captured for the very first time some knowledge of my jouissance in its absurd nonsensical reality gifted by my dream. I morbidly enjoyed being devaluated and my body indeed knew it. It carried those marks. Except that I did not want that at all! I want to enjoy dancing even if I err.

Desire

That dream marked the end of my analysis, and through its consequent articulations I experienced enduring effects. I love now in the way I desire, without the restrictions of my culture or the persecutions of my lineage. I found a way to rewrite the marks of my body. The experience of time changed. No longer nostalgic or future-oriented, work and leisure run today in a continuous almost undifferentiated line of a satisfying present, even when I am sad, jealous, or worried. While little dramas persist, my main concerns are no longer about my private misery, but the misery of the world we live in, and the necessity of creating less oppressive social links.

Loss

And I know about loss… and its true value.

Only You Would Dream of Such a Thing!

"Only you would dream of such a thing!": an interpretation aiming at the heart of the obsessional impasse.

Dream analysis holds a pivotal role within one's analytical journey, often marking its inception, guiding path, and sometimes its culmination. An analysis conducted through the lens of dreams is considered valid and conventional, aligning with Freud's foundational principles of psychoanalysis. In his seminal work, 'The Interpretation of Dreams,' Freud illuminated the notion that dreams illuminate the enigmatic corridors of the unconscious. However, misinterpretations occasionally arise from Freud's statement that a 'dream is the royal road to the unconscious,' erroneously implying that a dream solely represents the unconscious, rather than being one of many conduits to access it. Other manifestations of the unconscious, such as Freudian slips, bungled actions, jokes, and symptoms, complement this realm.

My personal analysis, predominantly driven by a series of dreams, taught me that a dream doesn't merely serve as a gateway to the unconscious; it can also pose an obstacle to its revelation. This realization stemmed from an interpretation that unfolded years after the initial stages of analysis. Here's how it transpired.

Being an obsessional subject, my analysis from the outset served the analyst, in service to the Other. Aware that dream exploration is an integral part of analysis, I began by dreaming vivid, almost self-explanatory material. Fragments from my day would construct compelling dream sequences, laden with potent imagery, marked by critical signifiers, offering glimpses into my history, distress, anxieties, and fantasies. I would dream, and the analyst would encourage self-interpretation. Rarely did the analyst interject with striking analyses or interpretations, yet I held onto the belief, spanning many years, that I was an exemplary analysand, dutifully adhering to psychoanalytic norms.

There's no need for additional proof to identify the core of obsessional neurosis; the obsessional embodies obedience, the good pupil devoted to the master. The obsessional's aim is to avert the emergence of desire, maintaining their relationship with the Other, akin to how it transpires in analysis, at the level of demand. The obsessional's fantasy is to be left in peace if the master is content. However, the analyst's role contradicts this notion. The analyst is tasked with unsettling the obsessional. The ethics of psychoanalysis, as expounded by Lacan, align with the

DOI: 10.4324/9781032637723-51

ethics of desire. Desire doesn't surface when the subject or the Other is satisfied; it emerges when lack is apparent.

My breakthrough from this impasse came through an interpretation of a dream by my analyst in the eighth year. Arriving at the analyst's office, as usual, armed with one or two dreams, I followed a pattern where dreaming compensated for my lack of verbal contribution in analysis. This strategy, a reflection of the obsessional's resistance to change, hinted that despite the appearance of a desire to progress, deep down, I sought stagnation. This instance revealed that dreams, at times, obstructed rather than facilitated access to the unconscious. One dream stood out, replete with intriguing symbols, notably featuring 'Muslim nuns adorned in green Indian saris and pointed pink hats'—a surreal, non-existent amalgamation. Striving to elaborate on this peculiar imagery through free association, I found myself delving into a labyrinth of associations, epitomizing the 'controlled delusion' inherent in analysis.

My analyst refused to engage in this attempt at interpretation, finally standing up and inviting me to do the same. With a statement—'Muslim nuns with pointy pink hats… only you would dream of such a thing!' At that juncture, a smile crossed my face, believing, somewhat foolishly, that the analyst was praising my adeptness in dreaming. Once again, I felt I had succeeded in pleasing the analyst, meeting their expectations by presenting my captivating dream. There seemed to be no hint of inadequacy or longing anywhere on the horizon.

It took a while for me to grasp that the analyst's response wasn't admiration but a reprimand. The focus wasn't on my brilliance but rather on my unwavering commitment to concealment—constantly furnishing the analysis with striking imagery and symbols, effectively barricading the pathway to desire. It wasn't a recognition of 'only you [possess the extraordinariness to] dream of such a thing,' but rather 'only you [would resort to such methods] to dream of such a thing [in order to evade discussing desire].' This wasn't commendation; it was disdain, shedding light on the fact that the obsessional tactics of evading the Other were transparent to the analyst. Several more years elapsed before dreams began to unveil rather than obscure, facilitating the analytical journey towards desire instead of catering to the obsessional's inclination for inertia.

My PIN

Beginning

I started my analysis ten years ago when I reached a level of suffering that was not tolerable anymore. I was going through a very painful breakup with a man I thought I could not live without. People say heartbreaks heal over time, but I wasn't healing, and the more time passed, I found myself more invested in my lost love. I was depressed day and night, having vivid dreams of him and waking up in the morning devastated that it was just a dream. I could not talk about this to family and friends anymore as they didn't want to hear about this man who hurt me so much, and plus, even if we talked about it, they weren't helpful, which was the first thing for me to learn from analysis – that it is not about being told what to do as the people around me were already doing that. I started thinking something was wrong with me. Someone who was completing their formation as a psychoanalyst at the time suggested that I see a psychoanalyst as perhaps there was something deeper than I needed to think about to help me understand why I had invested so much of myself in this man who had left me.

In the first few months of the analysis, it was just good to get things off my chest and have someone listen to me without guiding me to think in a certain way. It was interesting that I chose not to talk about the breakup for a while although this was my main reason to start analysis. The pain was unbearable to even describe: in a way it was crystallised and kept inside me as I talked about other things in my life, and it took me some time to even refer to the subject. That is why I needed a long-term approach, to allow me the time I needed to start speaking. I kept hearing from people around me something about 'transference', the unconscious connection to the analyst. I carefully chose my words; I was too conscious of how I presented myself or what I wore the day of the session. At the beginning, it was all about what the analyst thought of me rather than what I was saying.

The Couch Moment

Sometimes things can go unplanned and lead to changes in your analysis. One of these moments for me was trying the famous couch almost everyone asks about when you are in psychoanalysis. Not everyone in analysis uses the couch,

DOI: 10.4324/9781032637723-52

but nevertheless, something shifted for me when I made the move. I was at my analyst's door just minutes before the session, struggling with one of my contact lenses. It was so painful that I rubbed my eye briefly, but unfortunately the lens fell where I could not recover it. I had no choice but to remove the other one as I could not see properly. However, my vision was worse now. I entered the room and told my analyst what happened. All I could see was a blur. In this session, I felt I was more focused and spoke as if 'I was alone in the room'. My thoughts were just flowing, and at the end of the session, I acknowledged this to my analyst saying 'I spoke freely', and it was thanks to my contact lenses. Then my analyst said, 'Maybe it's time to try the couch'. It could not be clearer here why and how the couch is helpful in terms of free associating and speaking without looking at your analyst, fantasising about what they would say or think about you. It was the perfect moment for me to enter a different phase in my analysis, that is, from the analyst's gaze to my unconscious.

Articulation

My moving to the couch didn't mean that articulating was much easier. Thinking about the breakup, 'this man' was so difficult at times that I wanted to avoid talking about him. I started being sick often and missing my sessions. My analyst told me after a few cancellations that I need to start paying for the missed sessions. This intervention helped me to return to the sessions and face what was going on. Although I knew this was the right intervention (or fair), I was angry with my analyst who got me thinking more about what was keeping me fully invested in the past. The first five or six years of analysis, I had many other relationships where I could see something similar was being repeated, although with less impact than the previous relationship, and I always ended up getting upset with men.

The more I started realising and articulating the nature of these relationships and why I was holding onto the pain so dearly, the more it became a conscious process rather than something that had just 'happened to me'. When people say, 'Do you just talk in analysis?', they underestimate the power of articulating something known to them but that could lead to other revelations.

Analysis Is Not Just in the Consulting Room

I thought analysis is a once- or twice-weekly commitment, but it is much more than that, whatever the actual frequency of the sessions. An example that would best explain this is a conversation I had with my friend a few years ago. She asked me how I started my analysis and wondered about the breakup, and it suddenly dawned on me that one of my bank cards still had this man's birthday as my PIN. My friend commented that this was a good topic for my analysis that week. I thought about what the meaning of keeping this date was as a PIN. It had seemed insignificant to me during our conversation, especially as I had cleared out his things after the breakup, but I realised later how much meaning it was taking up in my mind and possibly holding me back unconsciously. This was the moment I realised that analysis takes place not just in the consulting room but also when you are not in the room. It is a psychical work in progress. Interesting moments and thoughts like these led me to eventually start my formation as an analyst.

Conjunctions of Embarrassment and Suffering

If I consider the premise of psychoanalytic interpretation to be the unconscious, I do not picture a (however faultily) locked vault containing and hiding true meanings. Rather, I think of some incorporeal barrier between my saying and what I've said, one which characterises any potential meaning as involuntary and erratic. From my speaking point of view, as analysand, entertaining the premise of analysability, the analyst's effort to interpret is less like digging into the depths than registering and perhaps reflecting, or making reflective, the opacity of this nonetheless ghostly barrier.

In my analysis, I have often brought, and continue to bring, material relating to embarrassment and to suffering. Looking at these words now, I find it plausible if not obvious to read 'embarrassment' as a specific form of generic 'suffering'. Taking for granted no such classification, however, my analyst listened to the repetitious, contradictory, delusory and implicating ways in which I used these words—as concepts as well as affects—for one year before she said[1]:

You link embarrassment and suffering.

This interpretation was a 'return to sender' seal: it induced the sensation of receiving one's own undelivered letter and seeing one's handwriting as another's. The effect unsettled something by being both surprising and deflating—and secondarily surprising for being both at once.

It was not that the words' proximity, even contiguity, sounded so foreign to me. It was not merely their being associated with each other that was unsettling. It was the coordinating conjunction 'and', and its encouragement by the verb 'link', that struck me. The 'something' unsettled was the character of their association, the logical relation between them that I'd assumed and operated under ignorantly, which would have been expressed with subordinating rather than coordinating conjunctions: 'although', 'unless', 'until', 'than', rather than 'and'—or 'or'.

For example,: I might be embarrassed, believing that X knows that I wanted to be chosen or seen by them in some specific way and, then, was not chosen or seen as I'd wanted to be—but I am more embarrassed by this embarrassment, which is so petty and vain in comparison with (less than) real suffering. Although I suffer

DOI: 10.4324/9781032637723-53

from embarrassment, the real sufferers experience something too profound too intimately to react with such myopic vanity. Until I'm beyond embarrassment, unless I lose that something in myself on behalf of which I am embarrassed, I cannot attest to true suffering.

Why it was so important not only that I had not and could not but that I should truly suffer remained unquestioned in this line of thought. But the replacement of 'unless' with 'and' led to an extended attempt to formulate and elaborate the logic in sentences. After much iteration and with the aid of further interpretations, I found myself articulating a fantasy from an oblique angle: 'I don't know how to want something that isn't noble and potentially catastrophic.' In turn, I could then ask myself: how does my embarrassment not only not undermine ultimate suffering but, precisely by undermining it at a certain level, how does it condition and sustain a particular notion and experience of pain—one not unrelated to punishment—that is crucial to me?

A saintly verse that echoes and occasionally surfaces in my mind says, 'Live in Hell and Despair Not'.[2] I would associate: If I live in Hell (I felt that I did) and I do despair, then I must not be living in real Hell, or I must not be really living in it. That is, if, in being embarrassed, I despair, and I despair in my embarrassment, then I cannot possibly know the Hell that would tempt me with despair; I must not even know despair. I was evidently caught in a circle, but always a lesser one, a less than truly vicious (virtuous?) circle. But, again, through further work enabled by the fateful conjunction, 'You link embarrassment and suffering', I was able to begin asking myself: to what end did I measure myself against this particular saintly mantra? More precisely, what was being served by my failure to live up to what I confusedly thought it meant? Structurally, I could reflect that only I had smuggled in the subordinating 'if, then' framework. In fact, 'Live in Hell and Despair Not' simply coordinates two imperatives.

In my ways of thinking, speaking and writing, I often rely on prepositional phrases like 'rather than', which negate and suspend the subordinate clause from the 'main' clause of the sentence. A persistent if unacknowledged tendency to hierarchise—connected to the possibility of making exceptions—lurks in this syntax. My analyst's interpretation acted upon this tendency by making it possible for me to encounter it when hearing my own syntax as absent in in the interpretive 'and'. Invoking the mere possibility of an encounter, prescribing neither what I would do about it nor whether I'd do anything at all, the interpretation reconfigured—at the same time that it, because it, reflected—the logical relations between 'embarrassment' and 'suffering' that I'd been unwittingly assuming, ratifying and obeying. In reflecting the fact that I 'linked' these signifiers, the interpretation presented their relation as *a posteriori* rather than *a priori*, related in time by me, not before time by an Other. Consequently, the future of their relation opened up.

To conclude, I must sharply distinguish what I encountered from what other therapies might call an 'unhelpful thought pattern' or an 'erroneous cognition'. By not presupposing the moral value of a thought or a symptom, the interpretation addressed not hierarchy or subordination as such but rather what kind of hierarchies my speech upheld and what their perpetuation might provide—and oblige. The interpretive 'and' could be transposed to coordinate self-preservation and self-undermining. In my relatively brief analytic experience, the 'self-' is less certainly evaluable than anything.

Notes

1 I only discovered this linear-temporal fact in the process of writing this piece by consulting hitherto unread notes written after each session. The emphasis of the interpretation highlighted and acted upon a rather more circular temporality.
2 For years I have misremembered the quotation from Silouan the Athonite, which I first encountered in Gillian Rose's work: 'Keep your mind in hell and despair not'.

Unconscious and Drive Being Cut

I remember little of what my analyst says to me.

This may bear witness to the intimacy of her words, which enables my unconscious to put them to work and interpret them. I would be tempted to say that her words are intimate to the point of being mostly unmemorable. This doesn't mean that they are unremarkable, or unprovocative, or without effect. Intimacy is the battlefield onto which she relentlessly sends me to face the real of my symptom and my ideals. A general with an army of one? She certainly shows little regard for the wounds that I complain about. As I wonder whether I am really consenting to all this, she reminds me that I volunteered for it. I puzzle over how you can both volunteer for something and not consent to it. Cut.

The cut unveils the formula of my symptom, volunteering without consenting. The cut of the session is always a wound for me. I'm confused. Is the cut the wound? Or has the cut revealed the wound? To this revealing, I timidly volunteer and consent. Cut.

She said to me, "Finally, you're actually saying something, after all these years." Ouch. To be fair, it's hard to make me say anything definitive. It's not that, as Lacan said, "I don't want to know anything about it." But I certainly don't want to know anything definitive. Jean Gabin sang when I was a child: "You never know the sound and colour of things, that's all I know." Metaphor is mundane. Metonymy is much more enjoyable. You can lodge the real in it and endlessly play hide and seek with it. Cut.

The cut unveils the drive. Last time, she asked me whether I had a fetish. I didn't know. Next time, I'll reveal to her that it is the gaze. Cut.

I am surprised to discover what I wrote about interpretation in my analysis. Perhaps this fictional account will illustrate how the unconscious interprets under the asemantic signposting of the analyst.

DOI: 10.4324/9781032637723-54

1982

After more than ten years of personal analysis, it dawned on me one day that something significant had shifted. I had embarked upon an analysis in the early 1980s when I realised that I had been depressed for about a year, and that, rather than lifting, the depression was tending to become more entrenched. It was as if a switch had been turned off. The initial effect was almost imperceptible, but over time it had sapped more and more of the pleasure and dynamic energy out of my life.

The analysis settled quite quickly into a pattern: averaging three sessions a week, a break over the summer, very little intervention on the analyst's part. There occurred a slow but steady attenuation in and emergence from the depressed state hitherto afflicting me. Alongside this, I entered into a formal analytic training course after about five years of analysis. Some years later I suffered serious injuries in a near fatal road accident. After a relatively short interruption, I resumed my personal analysis.

The accident coincided with the completion of the formal aspect of the analytic training. Over time I became more involved in the training programme. Alongside this, having experienced acupuncture and Chinese medicine as part of the rehabilitation process, I undertook a training in Chinese medicine. This has led over the years to a series of cognate studies; in medical Qigong, Tai Ji Quan, biodynamic craniosacral osteopathy. However, none of these has replaced psychoanalysis as the central focus of my activities.

The significant element alluded to above was the context within which I had experienced the depressive episode which in turn led me to seek a personal analysis. I summed it up in a phrase, 'That the sixties ended for me in nineteen eighty two'. The last gesture of the political activism which had occupied my time from the mid-sixties onwards was a six-week, twice-weekly seminar series, at the Institute of Contemporary Arts (London), in 1980. It was a critique of modern Irish nationalism, entitled 'The Future of a Different Past'. The hope, on my part and that of my colleague, with whom I had collaborated in developing the seminar series, was that it would kick-start the emergence of a new paradigm within the political economy of post-colonial societies. It was not to be.

DOI: 10.4324/9781032637723-55

A little over ten years previously, we were part of a research group which had changed both public perception and Irish government policy with respect to exploitable raw material resources, especially metals. Unfortunately, this was occurring just as the long post-war economic boom was coming to an end, compromising the benefits of possession of raw material resources, save in monopoly situations, such as The Organization of the Petroleum Exporting Countries (OPEC) and oil. By the early 1980s, Irish government mishandling of economic policy, faced with these circumstances, led to a deep, decade-long, economic recession.

This was the context within which the focus of my involvements shifted from political activism to the search for conceptual tools with which to address questions concerning the interweaving of subjectivity and society. In hindsight, the depressive episode could be seen as a phase of transitional mourning for the persona I had previously inhabited. In practice, I sat with the significant element for a time, before bringing it into the analysis. I suggested to the analyst that we continue to the end of the year (about eight months), to see what else might emerge. The analyst didn't express a view on the matter.

Since nothing of noticeable moment did emerge over that eight-month period, I again broached the question of whether or not we should continue. The analyst expressed the view that I could always engage in another tranche of analysis in the future. It was on this note that we finished, with the invitation to begin again ringing in my ears.

I have not yet taken up the offer implied in the interpretation, although I have a sense that a renewed consideration of it is drawing near.

A final remark, I have had two people come to me, after many years, decades in one case, of continuous analysis with their analyst before termination. Both, independently, have expressed surprise at how different the content they have brought, on this second occasion, to that of the first.

Index

For Product Safety Concerns and Information please contact our EU
representative GPSR@taylorandfrancis.com
Taylor & Francis Verlag GmbH, Kaufingerstraße 24, 80331 München, Germany